Strategic Studies Institute
and
U.S. Army War College Press

THE STRUGGLE FOR YEMEN AND THE CHALLENGE OF AL-QAEDA IN THE ARABIAN PENINSULA

W. Andrew Terrill

June 2013

The views expressed in this report are those of the author and do not necessarily reflect the official policy or position of the Department of the Army, the Department of Defense, or the U.S. Government. Authors of Strategic Studies Institute (SSI) and U.S. Army War College (USAWC) Press publications enjoy full academic freedom, provided they do not disclose classified information, jeopardize operations security, or misrepresent official U.S. policy. Such academic freedom empowers them to offer new and sometimes controversial perspectives in the interest of furthering debate on key issues.

*****

Comments pertaining to this report are invited and should be forwarded to: Director, Strategic Studies Institute and U.S. Army War College Press, U.S. Army War College, 47 Ashburn Drive, Carlisle, PA 17013-5010.

*****

The author would like to thank Dr. Steven Metz, Sarah E. Womer, and Mary J. Pelusi for useful and insightful comments on earlier drafts of this work. He would also like to thank James McCready for valuable support as his research assistant in the summer of 2012. All mistakes in this work of fact, omission, interpretation, and speculation are, nevertheless, entirely his own. All the information in this monograph is current as of February 2013.

*****

FOREWORD

In recent years, al-Qaeda in the Arabian Peninsula (AQAP) has been widely recognized as a more dangerous regional and international terrorist organization than the original al-Qaeda led by Osama bin Laden until his 2011 death. AQAP (which Yemenis simply call al-Qaeda) grew out of the original al-Qaeda group and maintains a radical outlook based heavily on bin Laden's extremist ideology. This radical group became prominent in the early 2000s when it began terrorist operations in Saudi Arabia, although it was ultimately defeated in that country. Following this defeat, AQAP retained its name and re-grouped in Yemen, merging with the local al-Qaeda organization operating there. In Yemen, AQAP was eventually able to present a strong challenge to that country's government. Over time, the group was also able to become almost totally independent of the original al-Qaeda, although it still preserves a public veneer of subordination. These developments, as well as the lessons from and future of the AQAP threat, are considered in depth in this monograph by Dr. W. Andrew Terrill.

Dr. Terrill uses this monograph to explore how Yemen's "Arab Spring" uprising paralyzed that country's government and shattered its military into hostile factions for over a year beginning in early 2011. This prolonged crisis prevented Yemen's government, under President Ali Abdullah Saleh, from doing much more than attempting to survive. Saleh used those military units that remained loyal to him for regime protection against anti-government demonstrators and troops who defected to those demonstrators. The uprising subsequently led to a security vacuum that helped allow AQAP and its insurgent force, Ansar al-Shariah, to expand their activities beyond terrorism due to the government's preoccupation with the Arab Spring. Although AQAP and the Arab Spring demonstrators felt no kinship towards each other, AQAP was more than willing to take advantage of the disorder produced by the uprising. In this new security environment, the militants were able to seize and hold significant amounts of territory in southern Yemen. Despite this focus on capturing territory, Dr. Terrill also notes that AQAP has remained interested in striking at U.S. interests in Yemen and especially in implementing spectacular acts of terrorism against the U.S. homeland.

Dr. Terrill pays special attention to the role of Yemen's current reform President Abed Rabbu Hadi, who succeeded President Saleh in early 2012 after a special election. In the war against AQAP, Hadi has made considerable progress, most notably by using Yemen's military to drive the insurgents out of their southern strongholds. In considering these events, Dr. Terrill provides a thoughtful and nuanced discussion of the controversial issue of unmanned aerial vehicles (UAVs), more widely known as drones. This monograph notes that both the United States and Yemeni governments now acknowledge that these systems are being used over Yemen, and President Hadi has discussed their use in considerable depth. While this monograph acknowledges many legitimate concerns about the use of U.S. drones in Yemen, it still clearly endorses them as an interim measure while the Yemeni military is in the process of reorganization and rebuilding. Dr. Terrill contends, however, that the long-term solution is the development of Yemeni military and police forces that can address all internal threats without depending upon U.S. assets.

Dr. Terrill further considers the problems that Yemen continues to face in restructuring its military and especially the ground forces so that they can contain, marginalize, and destroy AQAP as an effective insurgent and terrorist force. Many of his insights have important implications for the use of Landpower by U.S. partner nations. President Hadi's efforts to rebuild the Yemeni military have been particularly difficult because of the deep factionalism within these forces and the presence of senior leaders with deep ties to the old regime. Hadi, therefore, has proceeded forward in a serious but incremental manner. This is an important effort since AQAP remains a formidable force even after being driven out of the southern urban centers. Moreover, AQAP continues to strike at the government with hard-hitting raids and assassinations, and is clearly seeking to make a comeback in southern Yemen at some point.

The Strategic Studies Institute is pleased to offer this monograph as a contribution to the national security debate on this important subject while our nation continues to grapple with a variety of problems associated with the future of the Middle East and the ongoing struggle against al-Qaeda and its affiliates. This analysis should be especially useful to U.S. strategic leaders and intelligence professionals as they seek to address the complicated interplay of factors related to regional security issues, fighting terrorism, and the support of local allies. This work may also benefit those seeking a greater understanding of long-range issues of Middle Eastern and global security. It is hoped that this work will be of benefit to officers of all services, as well as other U.S. government officials involved in military and security assistance planning.

DOUGLAS C. LOVELACE, JR.
Director
Strategic Studies Institute and
 U.S. Army War College Press

ABOUT THE AUTHOR

W. ANDREW TERRILL joined the Strategic Studies Institute (SSI) in October 2001, and is SSI's Middle East specialist. Prior to his appointment, he served as a Middle East nonproliferation analyst for the International Assessments Division of the Lawrence Livermore National Laboratory (LLNL). In 1998-99, Dr. Terrill also served as a visiting professor at the U.S. Air War College on assignment from LLNL. He is a former faculty member at Old Dominion University in Norfolk, VA, and has taught as an adjunct at a variety of other colleges and universities. He is a retired U.S. Army Reserve Lieutenant Colonel and Foreign Area Officer (Middle East). Dr. Terrill has published in numerous academic journals on topics including nuclear proliferation, the Iran-Iraq War, Operation DESERT STORM, Middle Eastern chemical weapons and ballistic missile proliferation, terrorism, and commando operations. He is the author of *Lessons of the Iraqi De-Ba'athification Program for Iraq's Future and the Arab Revolutions* (Strategic Studies Institute, 2012), *The Saudi-Iranian Rivalry and the Future of Middle East Security* (Strategic Studies Institute, 2011), *The Conflicts in Yemen and U.S. National Security* (Strategic Studies Institute, 2011), and *Global Security Watch – Jordan* (Praeger, 2010). From 1994 until 2012, at U.S. State Department invitation, Dr. Terrill participated in the Middle Eastern Track 2 military talks, which were part of the Middle East Peace Process. He also served as a member of the military and security working group of the Baker/Hamilton Iraq Study Group throughout its existence in 2006. Dr. Terrill holds a B.A. from California State Polytechnic University and an M.A. from the University of California, Riverside, both in political science. He also holds a Ph.D. in international relations from Claremont Graduate University, Claremont, CA.

SUMMARY

In early 2011, the Arab world began going through a process of systemic political change that initially came to be known as the Arab Spring, although less optimistic references were increasingly used to describe these developments over time. In this struggle, which began in Tunisia and Egypt, a number of long-standing dictatorships were overthrown or at least fundamentally challenged by frustrated citizens seeking an end to corruption and the abuses inherent in an authoritarian state. Following the Tunisian and Egyptian examples, Yemen rapidly experienced serious street unrest that was directed at the over 30-year presidency of Ali Abdullah Saleh. Saleh struggled for over a year to maintain power but was ultimately unable to do so in the face of an enraged public and international disapproval for the corruption and violence of his regime. Under intense pressure, President Saleh turned over governing authority to Vice President Abed Rabbu Hadi in November 2011 under the conditions put forward by a Gulf Cooperation Council (GCC) transitional document. He formally remained president (without the powers of the office), until a referendum-type election confirmed Hadi as his successor. As President Hadi took office in February 2012, he faced not only serious demands for reform, but also a strong and energized insurgency in southern Yemen. The al-Qaeda in the Arabian Peninsula (AQAP) insurgency had no ties to the activities of the pro-democracy demonstrators, but it had flourished during the year-long power struggle in the Yemeni capital of Sanaa. Just as the AQAP insurgency was not linked to the pro-democracy movement, it was also not closely linked to the larger al-Qaeda movement outside of Yemen. Thus, with local leadership overseeing operations in Yemen, Osama bin Laden's 2011 death was not a serious blow to AQAP.

AQAP functioned primarily as a terrorist organization prior to 2010, but it later expanded its operations to include efforts to capture, hold, and rule territory in areas where the Yemeni government had only a limited ability to maintain security. This new strategy of seizing and retaining territory was implemented prior to the onset of the Arab Spring, although it was later accelerated due to the Arab Spring-inspired turmoil in Yemen. As Yemen became increasingly unstable, it was racked by violence between the regime and its opponents. In such an environment, AQAP used its insurgent arm, Ansar al-Shariah (partisans of Islamic law), to seize some promising opportunities to capture and retain Yemeni territory while the government was too absorbed in its own problems to respond in a decisive manner. According to a variety of sources, including Amnesty International, Ansar al-Shariah implemented an array of extremely harsh punishments for any action that was viewed as an infraction of their version of Islamic law. Such punishments included crucifixions, public beheadings, amputations, and floggings.

In his February 2012 inauguration speech, Hadi called for, "the continuation of the war against al-Qaeda as a religious and national duty." AQAP responded to his assertiveness with considerable ferocity by striking Yemeni government targets with suicide bombings and other acts of terrorism. These strikes were made in order to further challenge the government before Hadi could consolidate his authority. Even more significantly, AQAP won a major battle in southern Yemen during this time frame by attacking unprepared troops, most of whom appear to have been asleep after posting inadequate security. Despite this defeat, the government launched an offensive in the summer of 2012 to remove AQAP and Ansar al-Shariah from the territory they had seized in southern Yemen. The Yemeni offensive was conducted with a force of around 20,000 regular army soldiers, supported by significant numbers of paid local tribal auxiliaries. Saudi Arabia provided considerable financial assistance to support the operation, and it appears that a large share of the Saudi funds may have been used to hire the tribal militia auxiliaries requested to support the army. These types of fighters have often been highly effective in the kinds of combat that take place in Yemen. In the face of this attack, AQAP fought back proficiently and also conducted several spectacular terrorist attacks in Sanaa. Fortunately, the military prevailed against this resistance, and AQAP forces were ultimately driven from the urban areas that they had previously occupied.

In the 2012 government offensive, the international press reported the widespread use of U.S. drones, which, according to those same reports, may have tipped the tide of battle by gathering intelligence and serving to eliminate key insurgent leaders at important points in the campaign. While drone use has many political drawbacks, the possibility that it helped determine the outcome of the summer offensive is worth considering. If the Yemeni military had been defeated by AQAP in this effort, the government might have collapsed at an excruciatingly sensitive time, possibly leaving the country in anarchy. Such a defeat would also create the conditions for an even more deeply rooted AQAP presence in southern Yemen, with no countervailing Yemeni authority capable of moving against it. The success of the government's southern offensive would therefore seem to have been vitally important to U.S. national interests in the region. If Yemeni forces had failed, and particularly if they had failed ignominiously, a newly energized terrorist movement could have plagued the region and the world.

Unfortunately, despite the 2012 victory, the struggle for control of Yemen is still subject to uncertainty, and an AQAP insurgent comeback there remains a disturbing possibility. Moreover, the use of U.S. drones to ensure Yemeni security has already been seen to be deeply unpopular among many Yemeni citizens. Consequently, drones should not be treated as a long-term solution to that country's security problems. A more optimal long-term solution is a Yemeni military that is capable of maintaining national security without the direct involvement of foreign forces. Military reform, therefore, remains a vital aspect of dealing with Yemen's security issues. Yemeni forces are currently making some progress in this regard, and President Hadi has made a strong effort to modernize the military's structure and eliminate the warlord-style leadership of some Yemeni commanders.

During the 2009-12 time frame, AQAP also maintained a vigorous effort to strike against the United States, despite its increasing focus on expanding the southern insurgency, and then resisting subsequent government advances in that region. AQAP leaders considered terrorist strikes against the United States and efforts to defeat the Yemeni government as overlapping priorities despite the potential for a dissipation of resources with an overly ambitious agenda. Additionally, AQAP leaders did not seem to fear possible U.S. intervention with ground forces into Yemen in the aftermath of such a strike and may even have welcomed it. If the United States had invaded Yemen in response to a spectacular terror strike, it is almost certain that large elements of the population would have been willing to fight any foreign invader, no matter how valid the reason for intervention might have been. In such circumstances, the U.S. leadership would have an overwhelming need to strike back hard and might easily choose the wrong way of doing so.

U.S. support for Yemen at this time of transition remains important, and the United States must not regard the fight against AQAP as largely over because of the 2012 defeat of insurgent forces in southern Yemen. AQAP remains a dangerous and effective force despite these setbacks. Moreover, there are important reasons for defeating AQAP and its allies in Yemen, even if this does not destroy the organization and instead leads it to move operations to other prospective sanctuaries in remote parts of the world. Yemen is one of the worst places on earth to cede to terrorists due to its key strategic location, including a long border with Saudi Arabia. It also dominates one of the region's key waterways, the Bab al-Mandeb Strait which controls access to the southern Red Sea. Outside of the region, the problem of Yemen based-terrorism remains an important international threat which cannot be ignored.

THE STRUGGLE FOR YEMEN AND THE CHALLENGE OF AL-QAEDA IN THE ARABIAN PENINSULA

The U.S. military has also been working closely with the Yemeni government to operationally dismantle and ultimately eliminate the terrorist threat posed by al-Qaeda in the Arabian Peninsula (AQAP), the most active and dangerous affiliate of al-Qaeda today. Our joint efforts have resulted in direct action against a limited number of AQAP operatives and senior leaders in that country who posed a terrorist threat to the United States and our interests.

> President Barack Obama[1]
> June 2012

When the subject of Yemen comes up, it's often through the prism of the terrorist threat that is emanating from within its borders. And for good reason: Al-Qaida in the Arabian Peninsula, or AQAP, is al-Qaida's most active affiliate. It has assassinated Yemeni leaders, murdered Yemeni citizens, kidnapped and killed aid workers, targeted American interests, encouraged attacks in the United States and attempted repeated attacks against U.S. aviation.

> John O. Brennan[2]
> Director of Central Intelligence
> August 2012

The real battle against the terrorist al Qaeda organization [al Qaeda in the Arabian Peninsula] has yet to begin and will not end until we have eradicated their presence in every district, village and position; it will not end until internally displaced citizens are assured that they can return safely to their homes and organized terrorist operatives have surrendered their weapons and rid themselves of ideologies that contradict the sacred values of the Islamic religion.

Yemeni President Abed Rabbu Hadi[3]
May 2012

INTRODUCTION

In early 2011, the Arab world began going through a process of systemic political change that initially came to be known as the Arab Spring, although less optimistic references were increasingly used to describe these developments over time. In this struggle, which began in Tunisia and Egypt, a number of long-standing dictatorships were overthrown, or at least fundamentally challenged by frustrated citizens seeking an end to massive corruption and the other abuses inherent in an authoritarian state. In the face of these challenges, the Egyptian and Tunisian dictatorships fell rapidly and easily, thereby raising hopes in neighboring countries that their own ossified leaderships could be ousted as a result of an outpouring of street protests and other popular unrest. Nevertheless, when the excitement of these early victories over authoritarian regimes spread to other Arab countries, the revolutionaries were, in many cases, dramatically less successful than their counterparts in Cairo and Tunis. Unrest in Bahrain provoked a massive government crackdown which was assisted by other Sunni Arab monarchies in the Gulf and particularly Saudi Arabia. In the Levant, President Bashar Assad of Syria implemented a strategy of massive brutality against opponents in an effort to remain in power, seemingly at all costs. The Libyan regime also attempted to crush initially peaceful demonstrators by force, but it was defeated by an armed popular uprising backed by North Atlantic Treaty Organization (NATO) airpower and other forms of support. In the southern Arabian Peninsula, the flames of unrest also inspired discontented citizens in Yemen, where the Arab Spring quickly assumed many of the same features found in Tunisia and Egypt. Yemeni citizens staged massive civil unrest and called for the ouster of the regime of President Ali Abdullah Saleh. After over 30 years as president, Saleh's ability to survive in power was legendary, but the ouster of long-serving dictators like Egypt's Mubarak and Tunisia's Ben Ali clearly gave his opponents hope. The Yemeni leader strongly resisted calls to step down, but did not have the internal resources or foreign support to implement the same level of military repression as occurred in a country such as Syria.

Despite Saleh's strong efforts to remain in power, domestic and international pressures forced him from office in February 2012 for reasons that will be discussed later. While the regime often seemed anemic and frail, Saleh managed to retain power for over a year after the collapse of the Ben Ali and Mubarak regimes. During this time frame Yemen became increasingly unstable and racked by violence between the regime and its opponents. In such an environment, the terrorist group, al-Qaeda in the Arabian Peninsula (AQAP), used its insurgent arm, Ansar al-Shariah (partisans of Islamic law), to seize some promising opportunities to capture and retain Yemeni territory. This effort occurred while the government was too absorbed in its own problems to respond in a decisive manner. Throughout this period, Saleh often maintained that efforts to ease him from power could easily lead to sweeping AQAP victories throughout the country. While the doomsday scenario that Saleh predicted never occurred, AQAP did use Yemen's unrest to expand its control over most of Abyan province and parts of other southern provinces. In the summer of 2012, a new Yemeni government pushed AQAP and Ansar al-Shariah out of many of these strongholds, but the battle for control of Yemen is still subject to considerable uncertainty. An AQAP insurgent comeback remains a disturbing possibility. The context, history, and future of this struggle remain of tremendous importance to the well-being of all states concerned, with the threat presented by al-Qaeda's most dangerous affiliate.

THE CRISIS IN YEMENI GOVERNANCE

Yemen is a large and important country within the Middle East that has a long and porous border with Saudi Arabia and direct access to key strategic waterways, including the Red Sea and the Gulf of Aden. It is currently the only nonmonarchy on the Arabian Peninsula, as well as one of that region's more heavily populated countries with around 24,000,000 people.[4] The Yemeni population is currently growing by around 3.45 percent per year, and is expected to reach 38 million in the next 15 years.[5] Unfortunately, Yemen is also afflicted with numerous severe internal difficulties, and a large portion of the Yemeni population has problems with grinding poverty and malnutrition. Some sources state that the number of malnourished Yemeni children is around 750,000, with 500,000 of these children in danger of dying of starvation in the near future.[6] Yemen's 2011-12 civil unrest has also led to soaring prices for food and other staples as well as a breakdown of social services according to the United Nations (UN) Office for the Coordination of Humanitarian Affairs.[7] Increasingly, the UN specialized agencies involved with supporting Yemen have developed escalating concerns about the potential for a serious famine.[8] Water and electricity shortages are also common in Yemen, and the capital city of Sanaa faces the possibility of running out of water in the next few years. The water that is available is often unsafe to drink.

Yemen's most important political figure from 1978-2012 was former president Ali Abdullah Saleh, who left office in February 2012 as the result of massive and unrelenting domestic, regional, and international pressure for him to resign. Saleh had become the president of the Yemen Arab Republic (YAR-North Yemen) in July 1978 and then established himself as the first president of the Republic of Yemen which was formed in 1990 when North and South Yemen (the Yemen Arab Republic and the Peoples' Democratic Republic of Yemen [PDRY]) merged into one country.[9] Saleh's longevity in power and his considerable ruthlessness as president were useful, but never allowed him to establish himself as the leader of a powerful and efficient autocratic regime. Yemeni tribes were too strong and well-armed for this to occur easily. Reacting to his circumstances and limitations, Saleh ruled by manipulating the often competing concerns of Yemen's political factions, tribes, religious groups, and interested outside powers, including Western and Gulf Arab nations willing to provide economic aid. In this system, Saleh's primary approach to governance centered on his management of a network of patronage relationships and subsidies provided to friendly individuals, families, and tribes in exchange for their support.[10]

Saleh's government sometimes used repression to enforce its policies, but this approach was often a last resort which could not always be applied effectively within strongly tribalized regions. Saleh's Yemen consequently ran on a system of threats, subsidies, and bribes, with tribal leaders having consistently shown an interest in money that superseded concerns about religion, ideology, and politics.[11] Corruption permeated the system from the summit of political power down to impoverished junior civil servants or soldiers at checkpoints on Yemen's roads.

While Saleh's system of governance appeared unsustainable, the Yemeni leader managed to muddle through until the eruption of the region-wide unrest unleashed by the Arab Spring. To understand what is happening in contemporary Yemen, it is necessary to consider how Saleh lost the presidency, and what forces were unleashed by the revolutionary activity that eventually led to his ouster. As noted earlier, the Arab world experienced a political earthquake that began in 2011 with the unfolding of the Arab Spring. The rapid and spectacular ouster of the Tunisian dictatorship in January 2011 stunned the Arab world and raised the possibility that many other Arab regimes were not as deeply entrenched as they might appear. Tunisia's revolution helped ignite an 18-day upheaval in Egypt that led to President Mubarak's forced resignation on March 11, 2011. Many Yemenis observing these monumental events were deeply inspired by the Tunisian Revolution and then displayed an increased willingness to confront their own government after Mubarak resigned.

The crisis in Yemeni governance reached a turning point on January 20, 2011, when mass demonstrations against the Saleh government began occurring throughout many of Yemen's major cities. Like the Tunisians and Egyptians, Yemenis felt that their own autocratic regime had done little to improve their quality of life in 33 years. Also, as in Egypt and Tunisia, many Yemenis were angry about being victimized by the staggeringly high levels of corruption in their country during the years of Saleh's rule. Frighteningly, the regime's mismanagement and the economy's downward spiral had no obvious end since President Saleh appeared to be planning to install his son, Ahmed, as president when he finally did retire. Such a power transfer would have followed the emerging pattern of father-son succession set by Syria in 2000 when Bashar Assad succeeded his deceased father as president. This approach would probably have been replicated in Egypt and Libya had the pre-Arab Spring dictatorships survived in these countries. Additionally, before his removal from power in the 2003 invasion, Saddam Hussein appeared to be preparing his younger son, Qusay, to become Iraq's next president. This approach to governance was widely and derisively referred to as "republican monarchy" by detractors throughout the Arab world.[12] In this environment, the concept of a Saleh family dynasty was widely unpopular with many Yemenis, who were proud that they had replaced a monarchy with a republic in the 1960s.

President Saleh, despite his shortcomings, was quick to recognize the threat to his regime presented by the uprisings occurring elsewhere in the Arab world. Following the overthrow of Tunisia's dictatorship, he quickly moved to get ahead of the potential for serious unrest spreading to Yemen which had already started to experience large but socially narrow demonstrations comprising mostly university students and opposition activists.[13] As an initial move, he sought to shore up the loyalty of the security forces through a series of promised public sector pay raises and other benefits. Lower ranking civil servants were also promised increased remuneration to reduce the danger that they could become a source of discontent. In a move to contain campus unrest, Saleh exempted public university students from paying their remaining tuition for the year. Then on February 2, he announced that he would not seek re-election in 2013 when his presidential term expired and that his son Ahmed would not run for president.[14] This last set of promises, while seemingly dramatic, appeared hollow due to his earlier efforts to eliminate presidential term limits just prior to the outbreak of Arab Spring demonstrations in Tunisia and Egypt. Many Yemenis saw the effort to end presidential term limits as part of a Saleh plan to establish himself as president for life. They likewise expected him to return to that priority as soon as it was practical to do so despite any promises he might make at a time of crisis or political disadvantage.

Saleh's efforts to contain the unrest, while shrewd, did not prevent the escalation of demonstrations against his rule as he had hoped. Expanding demonstrations were increasingly difficult for the security forces to contain, and the Yemeni police began firing shots into the air in an effort to break up the unrest.[15] Additionally, as in Egypt, the government organized counterdemonstrations designed to show popular support for the regime and to confront the demonstrators, sometimes with broken bottles, daggers, and rocks.[16] This countermove led to increased street violence but in no way discouraged the protestors struggling against the regime. As Saleh's prospects for squelching unrest appeared to dim, opportunistic Yemeni leaders whom he had either bribed or manipulated into supporting him, started to distance themselves from the regime. These members of the Yemeni elite clearly had no interest in going down with a collapsing government. In the face of the expanding power of the opposition and the erosion of his own support, Saleh continued using what repression he could manage, as well as political maneuvering, to remain in power for as long as possible.

The situation then exploded. Regime violence against the demonstrators escalated dramatically on March 18, 2011, when the government used plainclothes rooftop snipers to fire into urban crowds as a way of breaking up anti-Saleh demonstrations. Fifty-two protestors were killed in Sanaa on that day, with serious casualties occurring in other Yemeni cities such as Taiz, Yemen's second largest city, 120 miles from the capital.[17] As the crisis continued, President Saleh declared a state of emergency, and for the first time deployed tanks into the streets to confront the demonstrators.[18] This massive escalation in regime brutality and killings split the Yemeni government. On March 21, Major General Ali Mohsen, the commander of the northern military zone and the important First Armored Brigade, changed sides and agreed to support the rebels. Prior to his defection, Mohsen was widely regarded as the second most powerful figure in the Yemeni regime. In accordance with the highly personalistic nature of the Yemeni military system, Mohsen's troops remained loyal to him after he broke with Saleh over the massacre. Additionally, a number of other senior officers, including three other brigade commanders, immediately rallied behind Ali Mohsen and also defected.[19] The regional and Yemeni media estimated that around 40-60 percent of the army had sided with the protesters, while some key units, including the Republican Guard, mostly remained loyal to the regime.[20] These troops had the best weapons and equipment within the ground forces (including Yemen's most modern tanks). Estimates of troop loyalty at this point in time must be regarded as rough, but do indicate a substantial division within the armed forces. General Moshen also pledged that his troops would defend demonstrators against regime violence.

In another blow to Saleh's hopes for remaining in power, Yemen's most powerful tribal leader Sheikh Sadeq al-Ahmar, head of the Hashid tribal confederation (Saleh's own tribal confederation), also backed the protestors. Sheikh Sadeq's brother, Hamid al-Ahmar, a multimillionaire businessman and important political leader, also emerged as an important source of opposition.[21] Adding to the president's troubles, a handful of members of parliament resigned in protest, including former legislative allies of President Saleh who were no longer willing to work with him. Surprisingly, Saleh appeared energized by his decision to make a show of strength on March 18 and was publicly unfazed by the defections. Rather, he unleashed a torrent of angry rhetoric against his opponents and seemed to take comfort from a large pro-regime rally in Sanaa that had been called in late March as a response to the activities of anti-regime protestors.[22] It seems possible that Saleh believed he had gained the upper hand at this point despite the defections due to his forceful acts of repression. He gave no sign of being willing to resign.

In this toxic environment, Yemen's Gulf neighbors became concerned about the escalating crisis in that country and the prospects for spreading instability. The leaders of the Gulf Cooperation Council (GCC) states led by Saudi Arabia rapidly came to believe that

Saleh would need to leave office for stability to return to Yemen. They may also have assumed that Saleh would prefer a comfortable retirement abroad rather than risk his life attempting to stay in power against increasingly long odds, and that he would therefore be persuadable. Correspondingly, in late April, the GCC offered a "road map" for Saleh's safe exit from power. The wealthy oil states within the GCC were among Yemen's most important sources of foreign aid and consequently could not be ignored. Saleh attempted to appear cooperative with the GCC leaders but was essentially playing for time and struggling to remain president. He promised to sign the GCC initiative on three occasions, but then changed his mind and refused to do so when the various promised dates for signing the document arrived.[23] The president's approach to the GCC Initiative was hardly surprising, due to his opposition to leaving office and his hostility toward the opposition. In April, Saleh made a speech at the Yemeni Military Academy where he stated that most of the opposition was composed of, "landgrabbers, smugglers of oil and gas, corrupt [officials,] and fraudsters."[24] He also claimed that the opposition was made up of "insurrectionists" who would drag the country into chaos.[25] Conversely, Saleh's refusal to follow through on promises to sign the GCC agreement only confirmed the opposition's worst fears about his intention to remain in power.[26]

Saleh also continued the brutality against street demonstrators and may have hoped that he could suppress the opposition to the point that international pressure diminished if he reestablished control over urban areas.[27] Yemen's second largest city, Taiz, was a particularly militant center of anti-Saleh activity and correspondingly experienced a great deal of punishment, including the use of artillery to shell residential areas where anti-regime rallies were being organized.[28] In Sanaa, there were also occasional outbreaks of fighting between pro-Saleh troops and armed members of the opposition, including troops loyal to General Ali Mohsen and tribal forces loyal to Sheikh Sadiq al-Ahmar.[29] Some of this fighting involved the use of rockets, heavy shelling, and machine guns.[30] These flare-ups were usually brought under control by hastily arranged truces.

Yemen's political situation changed dramatically on June 3, when Saleh narrowly escaped assassination as a result of a bomb explosion in a mosque inside the presidential compound. The president was seriously wounded during this incident, receiving both shrapnel wounds and serious burns. Additionally, several officials with Saleh at the time were killed and a larger number wounded. Saleh was flown to Riyadh shortly after the attack for emergency medical treatment amid speculation that he would not return due to Saudi pressure on him to step down. Some Saudi officials, speaking anonymously to the press, stated that the president would either remain in Saudi Arabia or settle in a third country.[31] Saleh's departure from Yemen and the possibility that he would remain in exile led to a lull in street fighting in Sanaa, but it did not last.[32] Moreover, if there was pressure on Saleh not to return to Yemen, it was not effective, and Saleh unexpectedly traveled back on September 23 to resume his role as president. He arrived on the 6th day of renewed fighting in Sanaa, which was the worst violence there since March.[33]

As the street confrontation raged, international opposition to Saleh's stalling tactics continued to mount and placed additional pressure on the Yemeni president to leave office in accordance with his earlier promises. The UN Security Council passed a resolution on October 21, calling upon Saleh to accept the GCC agreement immediately and resign.[34] Saleh could not easily ignore this development since the Yemeni economy depended highly on international goodwill and aid. Finally, on November 23, 2011, after a great deal of procrastination, Saleh signed the GCC initiative, and legally and bindingly agreed to step down from office in exchange for an opposition agreement not to prosecute him for any crimes that may have been committed while he was in office. The Yemeni president had struggled to avoid this outcome but also feared that any further stalling could lead to wide-ranging UN sanctions being directed at him and his family. Sanctions against individuals in cases such as these generally involve freezing their overseas assets and banning their foreign travel.[35] Moreover, protester demands for Saleh's prosecution for such things as ordering the use of deadly force against the protesters were sufficiently serious that the president may have decided to accept immunity while it was still available. It was also widely suspected that Saleh would have reneged on this agreement during the transitionary phase and remained in power if he had any opportunity to do so. Such an opportunity never arose.

President Saleh turned over presidential governing authority to his vice president immediately after he signed the GCC plan in November 2011. He retained the title of president as an honorific that would apply until the new president was installed by a referendum-type election (with one candidate) in February. As planned, Saleh was granted immunity from prosecution for all crimes that he may have committed while in office. Opposition parliamentary leaders, however, were able to restrict the level of legal immunity provided to the former president's relatives and close associates within the regime. These individuals can still be prosecuted on charges of terrorism, corruption, or the indiscriminate use of force.[36] Many Yemenis were disappointed that Saleh would not be held accountable for his actions including the crackdown on dissent and the use of rooftop snipers. Others believed that immunity was an acceptable price to rid Yemen of its strongman.[37] The agreement did not specifically demand that Saleh leave Yemen permanently, although U.S. Secretary of State Hillary Clinton later stated that there had been a quiet, informal agreement that he was to do so, which he chose not to honor.[38]

The GCC-brokered agreement contained a number of other provisions that went beyond Saleh's resignation. It specified that a new government would be formed with cabinet posts divided equally between Saleh's General Peoples' Congress (GPC) party and a host of opposition parties. The new president was to be Abed Rabbu Hadi, Saleh's long-serving vice president, who would be the only candidate in the February 2012 presidential election. The Yemeni Parliament had made the decision that political and economic conditions were too difficult for a contested election to occur. Instead, a caretaker president with a 2-year term would be installed, and the Constitution would be rewritten, with competitive elections planned for 2014. The details for approaching the task of the new Constitution are supposed to be worked out in a "National Dialogue" between the GPC and opposition parties which are organized in a coalition known as the Joint Meeting Parties (JMP). Hadi also promised to hold a referendum on a new Constitution within 18 months of his taking office.

Balancing Hadi's appointment, the new prime minister was to be opposition politician Mohammed Basindwa, a former foreign minister who had been a member of the GPC but then left the party in the early 2000s. Since leaving the GPC, Basindwa has been a political independent. He had also been strongly critical of the Saleh regime for the violence unleashed against civilian demonstrators and maintained considerable credibility with the Yemeni opposition.[39] Nevertheless, Basindwa's position as prime minister is clearly inferior in power and prestige to Hadi's position as president, and Basindwa has much less significance as a national figure. At the cabinet level, the GPC retained a number of key ministries including foreign affairs, defense, and oil. The opposition received the interior, finance, and education ministries.[40]

President Saleh left Yemen on January 22, 2012, for additional medical treatment in the United States to address lingering health problems associated with the mosque bombing in June. It is not clear how much overseas medical treatment was actually necessary, but many involved parties wanted Saleh out of that country during the election and while Vice President Hadi was preparing to enter office as the new president. In a speech given shortly before going to the United States, Saleh asked the Yemeni people for forgiveness for his "shortcomings" and stated that it was time for him to relinquish power.[41] More ominously, he also stated that, "I will go to the U.S. for treatment and then return as head of the GPC (which remained legal)," thus indicating his plan to continue to play an important political role in Yemeni politics.[42] He clearly meant these words and returned to Yemen on February 25, 2012, the same day as his successor was sworn into office. One day before the elections, Saleh had called upon his supporters to vote for Hadi, although this move was of limited significance, since there was only one name on the ballot.[43] Hadi thus was elected head of state but did not become the leader of the GPC, the political party to which he belonged.

Yet, if Saleh expected Hadi to act as a puppet, he must have been crushingly disappointed. Hadi seemed to understand that Saleh was now too divisive a figure to ever return to power, and, despite their many years together, he showed no interest in enabling him to do so, or to collaborate with him in leading Yemen. A central reason for Hadi's efforts to marginalize Saleh clearly involved the March 2011 massacre and the political significance of the blood on the former president's hands. In a statement that probably reflected more anger than accuracy, Yemen's Ministry of Human Rights released casualty figures on the total conflict in March 2012, stating that more than 2,000 people were killed in the turmoil surrounding the upheaval and around 22,000 were wounded.[44] This number was significantly larger than the over 270 killed reported by Human Rights Watch.[45] Both the Yemeni government and Human Rights Watch included a significant number of children in their casualty figures.

The Potential and Problems of the Hadi Government.

Yemen's February 21 presidential election was problematic since Vice President Abed-Rabbu Mansour Hadi was the only candidate on the ballot, and the process could therefore be viewed with some skepticism. Under these constrained circumstances, the most important question for the new regime's future legitimacy rapidly became what kind of turnout could be expected. Fortunately, the electoral turnout at 63-65 percent of registered voters was more than respectable, especially when considering that various groups—including secessionists in the south and the Houthi movement in the north—had called for an election boycott.[46] Following the election, Hadi was quickly inaugurated as president on February 25, 2012. At this point, a fundamental change had occurred in Yemeni politics. Whatever its shortcomings, the election confirmed Saleh's departure from office and his new status as an ex-president.

Hadi is a former general who, at 67 years old (date of birth, September 1, 1945), is only slightly younger than former President Saleh. He served as Saleh's vice president for 18 years, partially because Saleh wanted to showcase a few high ranking southerners (with no power base of their own) in a government dominated by northerners such as himself. Hadi grew up in the southern province of Abyan in the former PDRY and became an officer serving in the southern army when that part of Yemen was an independent country. In 1986, he and his troops fled to North Yemen in response to a *coup d'état* by military rivals in Aden. This coup was particularly bloody, and Hadi would almost certainly have been executed had the plotters been able to capture him. Later, Hadi's status as an exile changed when the two Yemen's merged in 1990, although he remained a loyal supporter of the Saleh government. This loyalty was underscored in 1994 when he played a prominent role in crushing the effort by southern Yemen to secede from the unified state.[47] Although one of the key reasons Hadi was initially selected as vice president centered on his status as a southerner, he remains widely distrusted in the south for his high profile role in defeating the 1994 bid to reestablish southern independence.[48] On the positive side, according to the *Yemen Times*, Hadi was widely respected at the time he entered office, "due largely to a perception that he kept his hands clean of political and moral corruption."[49] Some friendly sources also report that he distrusts tribalism and favors placing technocrats in high ranking positions.[50] While such statements sound like image polishing, they are also consistent with Hadi's upbringing in southern Yemen, where the Marxist government officially viewed tribalism as backward, although they were never able to rise above it.

President Hadi correspondingly did not begin his presidency with a strong, tribal, regional, or political power base, which may have been another reason that Saleh was comfortable placing him in his previous position of vice president. This weakness may also have been one of the reasons he was chosen as a transitional president, since various political factions may have assumed that he lacked the support to move beyond his constitutional role and attempt to establish a dictatorship. Saleh, for his part, may have viewed Hadi as a weak successor whom he could manipulate, perhaps through the GPC. As noted, Hadi is a member of the GPC, but Saleh remains the head of that organization. In March 2012, Saleh began using the GPC post as the basis for injecting himself back into Yemeni politics in ways that have troubled the Hadi presidency.[51] Early in the Hadi administration, Saleh was also described as holding almost daily meetings with security and political officials, despite his lack of any governmental position.[52] Some Yemeni observers even went so far as to call him a parallel ruler or even suggest that he was controlling key events behind the scenes.[53] Saleh was also reported to be making a strong effort to ensure that his own supporters remained in office and was sometimes described as ordering his loyalists to ignore Hadi's presidential decrees when they threatened the interest of regime holdovers.[54] To help bring this situation under control, the U.S. embassy in Sanaa issued a statement in March, saying that "it is not acceptable for any party to interfere in the implementation" of the GCC agreement. Saleh denounced the statement, which he correctly understood as directed at him and could not be separated from earlier threats of sanctions against him and his political allies.[55]

Hadi also inherited a governmental system with a significant number of Saleh holdovers in his cabinet and in other key positions throughout the administrative apparatus and security services. As noted, the GCC-sponsored power transfer agreement specified that the GPC would retain half of the seats in the cabinet, and some of these people were more loyal to Saleh than to Hadi. Moreover, during his time in office, President Saleh, like many autocrats, placed his relatives, as well as members of his Sahhan tribe (of the Hashid confederation), in a number of key national security positions in order to protect the regime. Some of these individuals remained in office for a while, although their political futures were clearly in danger. The most important holdover of the old regime was Brigadier General Ahmed Ali Saleh, the former president's oldest son, who remained the commander of Yemen's elite Republican Guard force for a while, although his command was eventually abolished, leaving his future in considerable doubt.

Yet, if Hadi's internal power base was uncertain, he has consistently received the support of Yemen's most important foreign allies. The GCC countries, which brokered the power transition agreement, are particularly important sources of foreign aid and investment to Yemen. Saudi Arabia has been Yemen's leading source of economic aid over the last several years and remains strongly involved with efforts to support the Yemeni economy. In the aftermath of Hadi's election, Riyadh has stepped up aid to Yemen to help the new government cope with its ongoing economic problems.[56] The United States, the United Kingdom (UK), and the European Union (EU) also backed Hadi and supported the GCC's Yemen Initiative.[57] Hadi's support from foreign countries concerned about AQAP can only increase as a result of his strong military efforts against this group, which are discussed later.

As the political break between Hadi and Saleh became more prominent, the former president widely denounced the government as "incompetent."[58] Some observers also suggested that he was working behind the scenes to undermine the Hadi government in the hopes that he could then find a way to return to power, following a Hadi failure.[59] Along with the EU and the GCC, the U.S. leadership took a dim view of Saleh's efforts to disrupt the Yemeni government. In response to the problem, President Obama followed up on earlier warnings and issued an executive order to freeze the U.S.-based assets of any individual who sought to obstruct the implementation of the GCC plan or "threaten the peace, security, and stability" of Yemen.[60] This order put a sanctions mechanism in place, which could be activated on short notice if necessary. While no names were mentioned, the order was clearly in direct response to the problems created by Saleh and his supporters. This action unquestionably strengthened Hadi's position.

Hadi's government, for all of its later strengths in fighting terrorism, has some clear shortcomings. As noted, the new Yemeni president has only a limited internal power base, and he has, therefore, on occasion attempted to expand it, using the traditional tools of patronage and favoritism.[61] This effort hardly reflects a fundamental change in the Yemeni political system and also may detract from any future effort at institution building. Likewise, the endemic corruption that helped produce the Arab Spring in Yemen and elsewhere remains largely unaddressed. Over time, Hadi and his successors may be able to do more to strengthen Yemeni governmental institutions if they wish to do so, but any such effort in the near future would probably be impossible due to Hadi's relatively weak position and the myriad of other problems he needs to address.

THE EMERGENCE AND DEVELOPMENT OF AQAP

Yemen, as well as Yemeni citizens abroad, have been prominent in the history of al-Qaeda and later its regional affiliate, AQAP, since the emergence of these terrorist groups as threats to Middle Eastern and global security. Among Yemenis and in the Yemeni press, AQAP is almost never referred to by that name. Rather, Yemenis almost universally refer to the AQAP organization simply as al-Qaeda. To many Yemenis, distinctions between al-Qaeda and AQAP seem artificial and unnecessary. There are some understandable reasons for this outlook. AQAP members frequently pledge loyalty to "al-Qaeda central," and the AQAP leadership had explicitly pledged loyalty to that organization, with bin Laden as its leader. Moreover, after an appropriately respectful period of time following bin Laden's death, AQAP leader Nasser al-Wahayshi pledged his personal and organizational allegiance to bin Laden's successor, Ayman al-Zawahiri.[62] At least at the level of formality and ritual, AQAP is a subordinate organization to al-Qaeda, although the truth is more complex, as will be discussed herein. Additionally, Yemenis and the Yemeni press seldom refer to AQAP's insurgent force, Ansar al-Shariah, as a separate entity. Instead, they describe these forces simply as members of al-Qaeda. As will be illustrated later, Ansar al-Shariah is not separate from AQAP. While Ansar al-Shariah acted as a front organization for AQAP early in its existence, this pretense has largely been given up, and its lack of independence from AQAP is no longer hidden.

Yemen has also been described as a near ideal jihadi sanctuary by a number of al-Qaeda writers from Abu Musab al-Suri to Osama bin Laden.[63] Numerous ideological and military works by jihadist strategists comment on Yemen's value as a sanctuary based on its large rural population, rugged terrain, highly independent tribes, and other factors. During the anti-Soviet war in Afghanistan, a number of young Yemenis participated in the fighting and entered bin Laden's circle of influence, often remaining loyal to him for years afterwards. Yemeni authorities usually viewed this situation as manageable and not particularly troubling in the short-term aftermath of their return. Throughout the early 1990s, Yemeni political culture viewed jihad against Soviet communists as a respectable undertaking, and returning fighters were often seen in a positive light. Additionally, many of the young jihadists had left Yemen due to that country's severe problems with unemployment, and Yemen's political leadership therefore expected that these individuals could be co-opted with government jobs upon their return. During this time frame, Western nations showed little concern about the actions of former anti-Soviet fighters, while other governments were also slow to recognize the potential dangers presented by Afghanistan veterans in Yemen.

After Yemeni unification, in May 1990, President Saleh viewed the Islamist veterans of the Soviet-Afghan war as a useful counterweight to southern Marxists in his political approach of playing conflicting groups against each other in order to remain in power. The value of these hardened fighters to the Saleh government later skyrocketed when up to three brigades of tough and experienced Yemeni jihadists were employed as auxiliaries of the Yemeni army during the 1994 civil war. This force made an important contribution to the rapid northern victory against southern secessionists, and many of the jihadists were rewarded with military, security, and other government positions after the war ended.[64] Others left Yemen, and some volunteered to join al-Qaeda in the ongoing Afghan civil war on the side of the Taliban.[65]

Some jihadists who remained in Yemen stayed in contact with other Islamist radicals outside the country and were interested in future armed conflicts that went beyond fighting Soviet and Afghan communists. Al-Qaeda, which is believed to have maintained a meaningful presence in Yemen since at least the early 1990s, was especially interested in striking at the United States. Their first terrorist attack against Westerners may have been a coordinated strike at two Aden hotels in 1992. These attacks were apparently aimed at killing American soldiers traveling to their duty station in Somalia, but instead killed an Australian tourist and two Yemenis.[66] Al-Qaeda's Yemen-based operatives are widely believed to have provided some support for the August 7, 1998, terrorist bombings of the U.S. embassies in Tanzania and Kenya, although no Yemenis directly participated in the attacks.[67] The most well-known attack at this stage of the conflict was the al-Qaeda strike against the destroyer *USS Cole* on October 12, 2000.[68] While the *USS Cole* was not sunk in the attack, it did have a large hole torn open on one side, and 17 sailors were killed, with 40 wounded. Yemen provided some cooperation in the U.S. effort to investigate the aftermath of this strike, but investigators viewed this support as grudging and circumscribed due to Saleh's efforts to avoid stirring up domestic unrest among anti-American elements of the population.

As the Bush administration considered whether Yemen was a potential security partner or an adversary in the aftermath of the *USS Cole* investigation, al-Qaeda carried out the spectacular strike against the World Trade Center's twin towers and the Pentagon on September 11, 2001 (9/11). Under these dramatically changed circumstances, President Saleh quickly understood that lenient treatment of Islamist radicals was now antithetical to his interests. Instead, he rapidly opted for an increasingly solid alignment with Washington in the struggle against al-Qaeda and quickly deported a number of foreign suspected radicals who had come to Yemen to study Islam.[69] Even more significantly, six al-Qaeda terrorists, including several key leaders in the Marib province, were killed in November 2002 in what the Yemeni government has now admitted to have been an authorized U.S. Predator drone attack.[70] Among the dead was Qaid Sinan al-Harithi, the head of the al-Qaeda branch which was then known as al-Qaeda in Yemen. By November 2003, Yemeni security forces had captured Muhammed al-Ahdal, who was then al-Harithi's replacement as the head of al-Qaeda in Yemen.[71] In 2004, with the al-Qaeda problem seemingly contained if not extinguished, the Yemeni government became much more focused on its conflict with rebellious Houthi tribesmen in northern Sa'ada province, while Washington directed its attention at problems associated with managing violence in post-Saddam Iraq.

In the aftermath of the 9/11 strikes, Saleh was forced to cope with an increasingly turbulent regional environment, including domestic discontent created by the U.S.-led invasion of Iraq. Like Afghanistan, post-Saddam Iraq became an important magnet and training ground for Yemeni radicals. The approximate number of Yemenis who fought in Iraq as supporters of al-Qaeda is uncertain, but many were given ample opportunity to wage war in that country if they wished to do so.[72] Some estimates suggest that as many as 2,000 Yemeni fighters participated in the fighting for the first 7 years of the war, but this figure seems high considering that the total number of non-Iraqi jihadists was seldom more than 300 at any one time, according to most reliable estimates.[73] Following this highly unpopular invasion, the Yemeni government chose not to challenge various radical clerics, including the prominent Sheikh Abdul Majeed al-Zindani, who openly encouraged young men to travel to Iraq to join the fighting.[74]

Difficulties with al-Qaeda forces in Yemen revived around 2006. One of the reasons most frequently given for this change is that a group of 23 experienced and resourceful terrorists conducted a mass escape from a Yemeni Political Security Organization

(PSO) prison in February 2006. The 2006 prison break has often been treated as the key event for the revitalization of an increasingly autonomous al-Qaeda in Yemen, but this evaluation is probably mistaken. In this regard, only a limited number of individuals were involved in the escape, and only of few of the escaped terrorists had much chance to cause serious problems after their escape. Within a year of the prison break, six of them were dead, and 11 had been returned to custody. Only six of the former prisoners remained at large in Yemen.[75] Consequently, however effective these remaining terrorists might be, there remains a clear need to look for additional factors in al-Qaeda's revitalization within Yemen. It is, for example, apparent that Yemeni jihadists returning from Iraq played a major role in revitalizing al-Qaeda in Yemen.[76]

Another factor of much greater importance than the 2006 prison break in al-Qaeda's revitalization involved the developments in neighboring Saudi Arabia in the late 2000s. By 2007, a number of experienced Saudi terrorists were making their way to Yemen following their defeat in Saudi Arabia, bringing much better financed terrorists into contact with the Yemenis.[77] The announced merger of the Saudi and Yemeni branches of al-Qaeda in January 2009, under the Saudi name of al-Qaeda in the Arabian Peninsula, was naturally of the greatest concern to the Sanaa government and underscored the danger of strongly revitalized radical forces in Yemen. Yemeni authorities responded to this new threat as best they could in the weeks immediately following this declaration, when the security forces rounded up 170 al-Qaeda suspects and other potentially dangerous radicals. These individuals were forced to sign pledges that they would not engage in terrorism and were then released to the supervision of their tribal leaders.[78] While the pledges themselves cannot be viewed as a serious deterrent measure, they were an unmistakable warning to the suspect individuals that they were under suspicion and could find themselves facing long terms of imprisonment (if not a death sentence) for future misbehavior. Likewise, the tribal leaders involved in this situation were required to guarantee the good behavior of these individuals as a condition of their release into tribal custody. Such actions may therefore have provided some limited value in preventing various radicals and malcontents from drifting into jihadist activities, but are probably of limited effectiveness in influencing the activities of hard-core terrorists.

Several U.S. and Yemeni estimates of the number of AQAP members at large were made in the 2010-11 time frame, and most of them placed that figure at 200-300.[79] By early 2012, the number provided by Yemeni sources had grown to at least 700, including members of the insurgent group, Ansar al-Shariah, which the Yemenis and others consider to be part of AQAP.[80] Even this larger figure has been proven inadequate and needs to be put into a broader context. In the past, such estimates included only full-time professional terrorists and not supporters or sympathizers who might be brought into the organization at a later time. Throughout 2011, an increasing number of AQAP's supporters and sympathizers seem to have crossed over to become actively involved in the military struggle against the Yemeni government under the organizational umbrella of Ansar al-Shariah. Virtually all serious observers will at least acknowledge that Ansar al-Shariah is affiliated with AQAP, and the Yemeni government considers it to be a front organization for AQAP. This monograph agrees with that evaluation and will later argue that Ansar al-Shariah is AQAP-dominated to the degree that it should be considered an arm of AQAP and not an independent allied organization.

AQAP insurgents in Yemen could number in the thousands, and provided the foot soldiers for the 2011-12 insurgency in southern Yemen. Some senior Yemeni military officers have also referred to Ansar al-Shariah as a "real army," which demonstrated courage and tactical skill during the time frame it was most active.[81] The 200-300 number mentioned above might also be dated, since it is often difficult to track AQAP growth, which occurs in two ways. The most straightforward way is when additional Yemenis choose to join AQAP or Ansar al-Shariah for whatever reasons might be compelling to them. These reasons include disillusionment and anger with the Yemeni government or with local tribal leaders allied with that government but also because there are financial opportunities for young men who choose to become fighters for AQAP.[82] The second way is for foreign radicals to leave their own country or previous foreign bases of operation and join up with al-Qaeda forces in Yemen. This process has often occurred in waves, most dramatically with Saudi radicals, but there are also recurring claims that radicals from Pakistan and Afghanistan have moved some of their operations to Yemen in response to problems they are facing in those countries with local security forces and U.S. drone attacks.[83] Other statements by Yemeni officials claim that significant numbers of Somali radicals continued to arrive in Yemen to join with AQAP.[84]

AQAP and Ansar al-Shariah.

The Western press has often described the insurgent force, Ansar al-Shariah, as "al-Qaeda linked" or an "al-Qaeda affiliate." More assertively, the Yemeni government has consistently maintained that Ansar al-Shariah is a branch of AQAP, and Yemeni officials and media often use the names al-Qaeda and Ansar al-Shariah interchangeably.[85] This Yemeni interpretation is clearly correct. After an initial period of ambiguity, AQAP acknowledged that it set up Ansar al-Shariah and controls this force, and no one from Ansar al-Shariah has disputed this interpretation. According to AQAP's then spiritual guide, Adel al-Abbab, Ansar al-Shariah was established by AQAP to impose the straightforward message that these fighters were struggling to establish the laws of God as a substitute for the corrupt misadministration of the Saleh regime in the territory that they had seized (in practice, portions of southern Yemen).[86] This emphasis on local issues was calculated to convey the image of an organization focused on fighting the corruption and brutality of the Saleh government in ways designed to appeal to at least part of the population. After Ansar al-Shariah was introduced to the southern Yemenis in this manner, the links with AQAP were to be allowed to become more obvious. Moreover, there was some hope that the message would find resonance, since the southern populations had little reason to be loyal to the central government. Rather, many southerners believe that government is not only massively corrupt, but also dominated by northerners who care very little about the south. It is also possible that AQAP sought to construct Ansar al-Shariah as a mass organization to make certain it was not left behind by the Arab Spring uprising in Sanaa.

This use of Ansar al-Shariah as a front organization was also useful since AQAP is often associated with a larger internationalist agenda, including striking out at Saudi Arabia, the West, and particularly the United States. Such an agenda, even if it appeals to some Yemenis, can also appear as a distraction from local concerns. Al-Qaeda and AQAP leaders have also worried about the possible tarnishing of the al-Qaeda name. According to declassified documents captured in the Abbottabad raid, bin Laden himself was personally concerned that al-Qaeda's name and reputation might have been damaged by the information campaign against it.[87] Such damage could clearly spillover to the regional affiliates who still pledge formal allegiance to the al-Qaeda core, sometimes called al-Qaeda central (a term bin Laden liked and adopted after reading it in the Western media). A related reason for the new name may be AQAP's concern about jihadist unpopularity in the southern part of the country due to President Saleh's use of Islamist fighters in the 1994 civil war. Many of these irregular troops had been involved in the anti-Soviet war in Afghanistan, and many had associated with bin Laden or his lieutenants. Thus, quite apart from international terrorism concerns, some southerners hold a grudge against bin Laden, al-Qaeda, and AQAP because of the actions of these fighters during the civil war. So, while Ansar al-Shariah appeared on the scene as a jihadist organization, its portrayal as local and spontaneous might have involved an effort to distinguish the front organization from some inconvenient aspects of previous jihadi history in Yemen.

Battlefield casualties are another indication of the overlapping relationship between AQAP and Ansar al-Shariah. In the aftermath of an airstrike against Ansar al-Shariah targets in mid-March 2012, Yemeni officials claimed that an important AQAP leader (Nasser al-Zafari) had been identified among the dead.[88] This event could be seen as further evidence of the interlinked relationship of Ansar al-Shariah to AQAP. Additionally, and perhaps more tellingly, significant numbers of foreign fighters have been reported among the Ansar al-Shariah dead.[89] The bulk of these foreigners are reported as Somalis or Saudis by tribal sources in the area. Such reports are not surprising. In February 2012, Major General Fred Mugisha of the African Union forces in Mogadishu stated that Somali radicals, and especially al-Shebab fighters, were fleeing to Yemen in large numbers because of their increasingly perilous situation in Somalia.[90] Egyptians and Afghans have also been reported to have been found among the dead.[91] It seems unlikely that these foreign fighters would find their way to Yemen in meaningful numbers and become part of a local group without international connections. Conversely, it seems much more certain that they could get to the battle front in southern Yemen by working through a group with powerful international connections such as AQAP.

Over time, AQAP's limited efforts to portray Ansar al-Shariah as a separate organization seem to have disappeared entirely. While Ansar al-Shariah initially flew its own flags, by 2012 there were numerous credible reports that al-Qaeda's black flag is being flown in areas controlled by Ansar al-Shariah.[92] If Ansar al-Shariah is a different organization from AQAP, they clearly have no problem flying this flag as though it was their own. Journalists who have visited these areas state that local people, as well as Ansar al-Shariah members, use the terms al-Qaeda and Ansar al-Shariah interchangeably. Another indication of the AQAP/

Ansar al-Shariah relationship occurred following a major disaster in February 2012 when Ansar al-Shariah defeated Yemeni army forces and captured a number of prisoners. AQAP entered negotiations with a variety of tribal elders on the possible release of these captured solders into the custody of their tribes, and with a promise not to "assist the enemies of Islamic law."[93] Ansar al-Shariah issued a statement that the release had been authorized by AQAP Emir Nasser al-Wuhayshi.[94] Their ultimate authority on important decisions was always the AQAP leadership.

AQAP and the Death of bin Laden.

As noted earlier, Osama bin Laden and al-Qaeda have a long history of involvement with Yemen, and many radical Yemenis have worked with bin Laden throughout his career. Additionally, a seemingly warm relationship existed between bin Laden and AQAP during the terrorist leader's final years, though actual command and operational links between al-Qaeda headquarters and AQAP seem to have faded to almost nothing by the time of his death in May 2011. This change took time to develop. Many of the Yemeni founders of al-Qaeda in Yemen (which in 2009 merged with the Saudi branch of al-Qaeda to form AQAP) fought with al-Qaeda in their youth and were devoted followers of bin Laden. The current leader of AQAP, Nasir al-Wuhayshi, worked closely for years with bin Laden as one of his most trusted and valuable aides in Afghanistan.[95] Moreover, Yemen was chosen as the site of one of al-Qaeda's most important early anti-American strikes, the bombing of the *USS Cole*. Al-Qaeda clearly dominated the attack on the U.S. warship, although it may have worked with a local radical organization (the Aden-Abyan Islamic Army [AAIA]). Bin Laden personally supervised the assault, including the choice of target, selection of the operatives, and funding of expenses.[96] He also overruled local suggestions that the best course of action would be to strike against a commercial ship.

After the 9/11 strikes, changes could be expected. Bin Laden's status as the world's most wanted fugitive would have made it difficult to exert any strong leadership role over AQAP planning, and he was consequently relegated to the role of an advisor and letter writer, who communicated sporadically and unreliably through couriers. While bin Laden's advice to regional affiliates may have been valued at some levels, he did not have the final word on matters of any importance. More likely, over time, the AQAP leadership probably viewed him as an out-of-touch nuisance, who had to be humored to some degree. This collapse of bin Laden's influence with AQAP was widely suspected prior to his death in Pakistan, but seems to have been dramatically confirmed by documents seized in the raid on bin Laden's compound. Some of these documents have now been declassified and provided to the Center for Combating Terrorism at West Point. While this information is incomplete, it has highlighted a number of interesting trends regarding the difficult and diminishing ties between bin Laden and AQAP. Among other things, the documents indicate that the al-Qaeda leader was upset and disappointed that AQAP had chosen to focus the majority of its effort on fighting the Saleh government rather than attacking the United States.[97] In addition, bin Laden's declassified letters indicated that he believed AQAP was making some of the same mistakes that al-Qaeda forces in Iraq had previously made. He was especially concerned that AQAP had attempted to seize territory without sufficient effort to gain the confidence of the local people, and that it alienated civilians with the noncombatant deaths it had inflicted.

Also, in a particularly revealing decision, bin Laden either sent or planned to send one of his most important subordinates (possibly Sheikh Yunis al-Muritani) to coordinate with both AQAP and al-Qaeda in the Islamic Maghreb (AQIM). In general, this visit seemed to be an effort by bin Laden to emphasize his priorities with the local leaders, but it was also something of a fundraising tour. While there is no record of the messenger being asked to solicit funds from AQAP, he was asked to request 200,000 Euros from the usually well-funded AQIM.[98] Such a request suggests that bin Laden was not supporting the regional affiliates with funding, at least by the time of the request, unless AQIM and AQAP were being treated radically differently. His likely inability or unwillingness to provide funds would have denied him an important instrument, which could otherwise be used to influence AQAP and the other affiliates. Without funds to provide to AQAP, bin Laden had almost nothing to offer that organization, and ignoring his advice was largely without consequences.

Surprisingly, bin Laden held AQAP propagandist and planner Anwar al Awlaki in low esteem, and was particularly distressed over the suggestion that Awlaki might at some point become the leader of AQAP. This concern was apparently not alleviated by Awlaki's internet advocacy of the importance of striking at the United States, as well as local Yemeni forces.[99] Bin Laden's reservations about Awlaki may have had something to do with their lack of personal relationship, or there might have been as yet unclarified differences between them on substantive issues. It is also possible that bin Laden was somewhat irritated with the tremendous amount of media coverage that Awlaki received, perhaps fearing that it would eclipse his own. As noted, bin Laden loved the term "al-Qaeda central," and could not be expected to take to the idea that others had overshadowed him within the world of radical jihadists. This concern would be especially clear in the case of Awlaki, who never met bin Laden and could not be viewed as a bin Laden protégé.

Bin Laden's death seems to have helped to accelerate the decline of al-Qaeda central and ended whatever residual influence that organization had over offshoot organizations, including AQAP. Unfortunately, it was not a serious blow to AQAP itself. Bin Laden's intermittent advice was almost certainly of little to no interest to AQAP (since they usually did not follow it), and his apparent inability to provide funds to AQAP meant that he had nothing of tangible value to offer to their cause. After he was killed, he also became a martyr to the al-Qaeda cause and could therefore be held up as a source of inspiration to AQAP members and potential recruits. Additionally, in a highly symbolic but probably operationally meaningless gesture, the AQAP leadership, as noted, has sworn loyalty to bin Laden's successor, Ayman al-Zawahiri.

The Emergence of an AQAP-Led Insurgency in Southern Yemen.

AQAP functioned primarily as a terrorist organization prior to 2010, but it later expanded its operations to include efforts to capture, hold, and rule territory in areas where the Yemeni government had only a limited ability to maintain security. This new strategy of seizing and retaining territory was implemented prior to the uprising in Tunisia and the onset of the Arab Spring, although it was later accelerated due to the Arab Spring-inspired turmoil in Yemen. One of the earliest indications of AQAP's increased willingness to fight as an insurgent force can be seen during the August 2010 combat operations in the southern town of Loder, which is around 150 kilometers (95 miles) northeast of Zinjibar, the provincial capital of Abyan province. Once the insurgents captured territory, the population was almost always subjected to heavy political indoctrination, based on the favored AQAP/Ansar al-Shariah question, "Why do you oppose being ruled by the law of God?"

Unfortunately for AQAP, no propaganda effort was likely to make their rule palatable to many independent-minded Yemeni tribesmen. The form of Shariah law imposed by this group stressed harsh "Islamic punishments" for any transgression that the group perceives to have occurred. One Ansar al-Shariah leader is reported to have stated that their objective was, "to apply God's laws in Abyan, the Taliban way."[100] This goal was apparently fully met in Yemeni territory controlled by AQAP/Ansar al-Shariah. According to a variety of sources, including Amnesty International, Ansar al-Shariah implemented an array of extremely harsh punishments for any action that was viewed as an infraction of their version of Islamic law. Such punishments included crucifixions, public beheadings, amputations, and floggings.[101] One woman was even executed for "sorcery."[102] Moreover, while it is possible that government-friendly media in Yemen exaggerated the brutality of Ansar al-Shariah, stories told by refugees from these towns overlap a great deal, and many Western and regional reporters have talked to anonymous refugees who have no reason to lie on behalf of the government. Indeed, many, if not most, southerners are critical of the government.[103]

In one of their earliest insurgent successes, AQAP/Ansar al-Shariah established a strong presence in Loder, which the Yemeni army chose to contest in August 2010.[104] As part of their new strategy, AQAP forces initially remained in Loder to fight against Yemeni military forces rather than attempting to escape with departing civilians. These actions indicated a level of commitment to their cause, as well as perhaps some degree of contempt for the quality of Yemeni military forces. Government forces ultimately won the battle in Loder and regained control of the town after several days of fighting, when at least some AQAP members escaped.[105] Heavy casualties were not reported on either side, perhaps indicating that AQAP did not view Loder as important enough to initiate a bloody last stand of the fighters involved.[106] Such a departure was probably reasonable, since the Yemeni government would always have the option of using artillery, airpower, and perhaps tanks to retake the town. After the battle, the citizens of Loder clearly did not want AQAP back, and formed armed resistance committees in 2011 to prevent AQAP from again seizing the town. The catalyst for the formation of the committees was the capture of the nearby city of Zinjibar by the militants in that time frame, and the concern that AQAP was once again expanding its territorial holdings.[107] These committees effectively defended Loder on a number of future occasions, when AQAP attempted to recapture the city but failed to do so.[108] After tasting Ansar al-Shariah rule, the citizens of Loder were clearly willing to fight ferociously to prevent a new AQAP takeover of their small city.

Elsewhere, in September 2010, Yemeni army units were again engaged in urban combat against al-Qaeda forces.[109] This time the fight flared up in the town of Hawta, which has a population of around 20,000. At least 8,000 of these people (and possibly a great deal more) were able to flee the village during the fighting.[110] Many others were prevented from escaping by the insurgents, so that their presence could help shield the terrorists from artillery and airstrikes while complicating the tactical operations of the Yemeni ground forces.[111] Such actions may have been precisely the type of behavior that bin Laden and other international jihadist leaders had warned AQAP to avoid if it wanted to gain the loyalty of the population. This encounter was also reported to have involved Yemeni army tanks and armored vehicles moving against an uncertain number of AQAP members.

In the 2010 fighting, AQAP showed its evolution as an insurgent organization through the ability to ambush or attack squad, platoon, and perhaps larger units of the Yemeni army. Police units were also regularly attacked.[112] In one September 2010 incident in the provincial capital of Zinjibar, al-Qaeda attackers on motorbikes used hit-and-run tactics against two separate police targets, indicating careful planning and effective execution of a synchronized mission. In September 2010, AQAP also issued a "death list" that included the names of 55 military, judicial, and police officials targeted for assassination.[113] Such lists are a common feature of insurgencies, and they serve as a warning that the named officials must resign their posts or face the possibility of being murdered. Adding to the uncertainty has been al-Qaeda's history of killing or kidnapping a number of very senior security officials throughout the country, suggesting that anyone they target may be vulnerable.[114]

In the aftermath of AQAP's withdrawal from Loder, there remained some positive signs regarding Yemen's efforts to control terrorism. In the summer of 2010, some of Yemen's tribal leaders in the areas south and east of Sanaa seemed to be reevaluating their views on the costs and benefits of sheltering al-Qaeda suspects in their areas. The harboring of such fugitives led to Yemeni military raids into their territory, and threatened to disrupt any patronage networks providing funds from Sanaa or Riyadh. Thus, both a key source of tribal income and overall security within tribal areas were threatened. In response to this evolving situation, tribal leaders from the important Abida and al-Ashraf tribes pledged that they would "stop harboring people wanted by the security forces or who are accused of belonging to al-Qaeda."[115] These pledges were interesting and positive developments, but not particularly surprising, since virtually no tribal leaders wish to see a new source of authority in their regions that might displace them. While certain tribal leaders have often been willing to shelter AQAP members for money, they have never been interested in ceding their authority to this group. Yet, seizing such authority from tribal leaders was now clearly understood to be an AQAP goal.[116]

The progress that AQAP made in its ability to deploy its insurgent forces dramatically escalated following the split within the army over civilian deaths in the March 2011 massacre of peaceful demonstrators in Sanaa and other cities. Ansar al-Shariah captured the southern city of Jaar in March and Zinjibar in May 2011, displacing thousands of residents.[117] This battle involved one of the earliest known insurgent uses of the name, Ansar al-Shariah. On this occasion, the insurgents flew white banners with the words, "Ansar al-Shariah," written on them and did not fly al-Qaeda flags as they were to do later.[118] Around 1,000 militants were reported to have seized Zinjibar after coming from Jaar, which had previously fallen to AQAP forces. The Yemeni army's 25th Mechanized Brigade was reported to have resisted the Islamists but was unable to prevent the city from being captured.[119] The 25th Brigade remained stationed near Zinjibar, but mostly conducted defensive operations in the aftermath of the defeat.[120] The insurgents came close to overrunning this unit in July 2011, but government forces managed to fend off the attacks with the support of air force units that were identified publicly as Yemeni, but were widely suspected of including U.S. drones or cruise missiles.[121] Yemen's Deputy Information Minister stated that the United States has provided unspecified "logistical support" for the 25th Brigade in order for it to cope with the insurgent siege.[122]

Offensive operations by the 25th Brigade in 2011 consisted mostly of shelling the insurgents with artillery. There were also at least three efforts to use tribal mediators to get the insurgents to withdraw from the city without further violence.[123] The government's heavy use of artillery and air power may have led to a significant level of civilian collateral damage at various points in the campaign.[124] While it would seem easy to criticize the brigade's leadership for lacking an offensive spirit, it should be understood that they were coping with serious problems in supplying their troops, due to the chaos permeating the Yemeni governmental system at this time. Logistical efforts from Sanaa could not occur due to the unrest, and Ansar al-Shariah cut off the supply route from the nearby southern city of Aden to complete the brigade's isolation. Under these circumstances, 25th Brigade leaders may have feared initiating offensive actions that they could not finish. Ansar al-Shariah, therefore, remained in control of Zinjibar, Jaar, and other areas in the rural south without serious offensive actions leveled against them on the ground throughout the remainder of Saleh's presidency. The military actions that did occur, for the most part, came from the air.

As President Hadi took office, he faced a strong and energized insurgency that had flourished after the year-long power struggle in Sanaa. When asked about his unit's situation in January, a Yemeni army lieutenant stationed in the south stated, "We are like an island in a sea of al-Qaeda. We are surrounded in every direction."[125] Under these circumstances, the Yemeni press worried that AQAP would make even more progress in capturing territory in the south.[126] These concerns were reasonable. In mid-January 2012, around 200 militants seized control of Rida, a town of around 60,000 people, about 100 miles south of Sanaa.[127] They remained in control of the town for only about 10 days. During that time, relatively few people seem to have been killed although about 10 police officers were reported to have been abducted, and around 100 prisoners were released from the Rida central prison, including members of AQAP.[128] It appears possible that local authorities struck a deal whereby AQAP could enter the town, release its prisoners, and then leave. It is also possible that the AQAP forces understood that they did not have a large enough force in the town to retain control if the townspeople were roused against them.

By February 2012, both sides were expecting the conflict to escalate. President Hadi had taken a clear hard line against AQAP as he entered the office of the presidency, and they had responded with considerable ferocity by striking Yemeni government targets with suicide bombings and other acts of terrorism. These strikes were made in order to create government failures before Hadi could consolidate his authority. In his inauguration speech, Hadi called for "the continuation of the war against al-Qaeda as a religious and national duty."[129] The challenge President Hadi faced from AQAP was violently asserted just hours after he took office on February 26, when a double suicide car bombing led to the deaths of 26 people outside a Republican Guard compound in the southern city of Mukalla.[130] At least 20 of the dead were soldiers.[131]

Moreover, by the time Hadi assumed office, the situation in the south was extremely precarious. Ansar al-Shariah forces had previously taken control of Zinjibar in September 2011, although they had failed to seize the military facilities outside of the city which remained under the control of the 25th Mechanized Brigade. The commander of that unit told a pan-Arab newspaper by telephone that Yemeni army forces attempting to resupply them had been ambushed and defeated, but the troops were able to hang on because the United States had sent some of its aircraft to airdrop food and supplies.[132] Later, AQAP spokesman Fahd al-Qusa claimed that the Yemeni military was only able to continue operations because of the support it received from U.S. air assets, including drones.[133] Qusa then admitted that the government had been able to open a road to supply the 25th Mechanized Brigade, and this resupply effort allowed it to avoid collapse. Qusa had sometimes been identified as AQAP's third in command. Somewhat ironically, the press would later report that he had been killed by a U.S. drone.[134]

The 2012 Government Offensive in Abyan Province and Beyond.

As he prepared to assume the presidency, Abed Rabbu Hadi promised to intensify the war against AQAP and destroy that organization's power within Yemen. This was an ambitious agenda, since the 2011 split in the Yemeni security forces between pro-Saleh and anti-Saleh forces created a security vacuum which AQAP was able to exploit to capture territory in the south. Now, a new government appeared interested in moving forward, although problems remained due to the continuing divisions within the armed forces. Many of these loyalists expected Hadi to allow them to stay in their positions, while their critics demanded that they be removed. Hadi initially retained a number of Saleh loyalists in office, although he was at least able to remove some of the military leaders he regarded as most untrustworthy or corrupt. Still, he could not wait to restructure the military or heal its divisions before moving forward in the war against AQAP.

Unfortunately, Hadi's war against AQAP did not start out well. On February 18, 2012, about 1 week before Hadi was inaugurated, but well after Saleh had relinquished actual presidential power to Hadi, Yemen's army suffered a staggering defeat at the hands of Ansar al-Shariah. At least 185 troops were killed when Ansar al-Shariah forces attacked a southern military encampment at dawn and killed a number of soldiers, many while they slept.[135] There also were around 70 Yemeni soldiers captured in the fighting, including approximately seven officers.[136] Ansar al-Shariah further captured a significant amount of equipment from Yemeni forces, including artillery pieces and armored vehicles. In the aftermath of the battle, Ansar al-Shariah forces paraded some of this equipment through the streets of Jaar as a celebration of the victory.[137] Photographs of Ansar al-Shariah fighters posing with these weapons were posted on jihadist websites and subsequently republished by the Yemeni and other Arab media.[138]

Some Yemeni citizens, furious about the defeat, charged that the disaster occurred because of the actions of incompetent or collaborationist army officers who had failed to take the proper precautions. Various critics also maintained that local commanders had struck long-term agreements with local insurgent leaders which served as informal cease-fires.[139] While insurgent forces may have honored these agreements for a while, they seem to have been used to lull the local army units into a state of complacency. Such actions would have created the conditions for AQAP to set a deadly trap. Moreover, while army losses were heavy, only 32 Ansar al-Shariah fighters were killed in the battle. Some prisoners also appear to have been released in what may have been an effort to accommodate various Yemeni tribes after mediation by religious scholars and tribal elders.[140] Also, and perhaps more importantly, lenient treatment of prisoners may have been used to give Yemeni forces an important incentive to surrender in future battles. If AQAP ordered all of their captives killed or savagely mistreated them, more Yemeni government troops might well fight to the death in all future combat.

Unsurprisingly, the AQAP leadership showed no interest in relaxing their struggle following their victory against the Yemeni army in the south. Less than 2 hours after Hadi was inaugurated, a suicide bomber rammed a Toyota truck into the wall of a presidential residence protected by Republican Guard troops in the southern city of Mukalla.[141] Twenty-six people within the compound were killed, including a number of guardsmen. AQAP insurgents also began striking against army garrisons in the south with hit-and-run raids. Yemeni officials admitted that the insurgents had seized armored vehicles, artillery pieces, and small arms during some of these attacks, in addition to the equipment captured following the February 18 battle.[142]

After the February defeats, the Yemeni military began to improve its performance in partial response to these hard lessons. Around 200 of Yemen's antiterrorist Special Forces were deployed into the contested areas to help local forces that were resisting Ansar al-Shariah.[143] According to the *Yemen Post*, these counterterrorism forces were sent to bolster government forces in Loder, which remained a key target for Ansar al-Shariah forces.[144] As discussed earlier, local tribal resistance committees were heavily involved in the defense of Loder, and participated in a great deal of the heaviest fighting in coordination with army units. Tribal officials claimed that the Yemeni army provided them with weapons, and it is possible that tribal forces from outside the city also received money to participate in the fighting.[145] Additionally, artillery and units of Yemen's air force were used against the insurgents, while many journalists expressed their strong belief that U.S. drones had also been deployed in strikes against insurgent forces.[146] Under these conditions, Loder was effectively defended, and insurgents were unable to capture it a second time.

Other problems followed for the insurgents. On May 6, 2012, senior AQAP leader Fahd al-Qusa was killed in what the Yemeni government referred to as an air strike, although the world press usually identified the incident as a missile strike by a U.S. drone.[147] Al-Qusa was a former associate of bin Laden who was wanted by the U.S. Federal Bureau of Investigation for his involvement in the 2000 attack on the *USS Cole*. He made serious mistakes in the attack on the *USS Cole*, although he may have gained some skill and sophistication as a terrorist leader over time.[148] He was also one of the few AQAP members involved in the 2006 prison break who was still alive and active in terrorism by early 2012. The death of such a well-known AQAP leader on the verge of an important offensive may have provided a potential advantage to the Yemeni government by eliminating a well-placed field commander. Seeking vengeance, AQAP quickly responded to Qusa's death by attacking a Yemeni military base near Zinjibar, with inconclusive results. Journalistic sources maintain that extensive use of drones just prior to Hadi's planned May offensive helped to gather useful intelligence, and disrupted the AQAP command and control by eliminating high value targets. Qusa, despite the mistakes in his early career, may have been considered a high value target.

On May 12, 2012, following the earlier effort to prepare the battlefield, Yemeni military forces launched Hadi's much anticipated offensive to recapture AQAP controlled areas in the Abyan and Shabwa provinces. The Yemeni offensive was conducted with a force of around 20,000 regular army soldiers, supported by significant numbers of paid local tribal auxiliaries.[149] U.S. military advisors were reported to have helped the Yemeni forces with planning the offensive, and Saudi

Arabia provided considerable financial assistance to support the operation.[150] It appears that a large share of the Saudi funds may have been used to hire tribal militia auxiliaries to support the army. These types of fighters have often been highly effective in this kind of combat in Yemen.[151] A number of tribes have a long history of accepting money from Saudi Arabia, and would have no problem accepting government funds to fight against AQAP.[152]

Just as importantly, Yemen's air force appeared to have been deployed with much greater intensity.[153] However, there is some doubt as to how much of the air effort was actually carried on by the Yemeni air force, and how much came from outside sources. Journalist sources noted what they called, "the government's routine insistence that only its aircraft carry out such operations on Yemeni soil," but they did not take such denials seriously.[154] Rather, virtually the entire Yemeni and international press corps seemed to assume that the increasingly effective air support was mostly provided by U.S. drone aircraft and missiles launched from U.S. warships.[155] Journalists from both the United States and Yemen claim to have spoken to a wide range of U.S. and Yemeni officials and also point to the extensive use of airpower in the campaign against AQAP. Observers often stress that Yemen's air force has only limited capabilities under the most optimal conditions, and operational readiness at the time (including recovering from a recent air force mutiny and work strike) were hardly optimal.[156] Other observers also suggest that the U.S. drone campaign was too large and significant to be kept a secret.

As the southern offensive continued, AQAP again struck back quickly and painfully against the government with a May 12, 2012, suicide attack against a military parade rehearsal at Sabeen Square in Sanaa, in which around 96 people were killed and 300 wounded.[157] The Yemeni defense minister, who was scheduled to visit the rehearsal, was late, and therefore spared the possibility of being killed in the bombing. The attacker was a suicide bomber dressed in a Central Security Force (CSF) uniform who managed to work his way into the ranks of the soldiers getting ready for the rehearsal.[158] AQAP claimed that action was, "only the beginning of jihad."[159]

Fortunately, the horrific attack in Sabeen Square did nothing to slow the southern offensive. Yemeni ground forces repeatedly attacked targets in or near Zinjibar throughout the first month of the fighting. The push against the provincial capital was described by Yemeni officials as a "wide offensive" that involved military pressure being directed against the city from three sides, using elements of the army, air force, and tribal militias. Elements of the Yemeni navy were involved in the offensive, and may have played a useful supporting role since Zinjibar is a coastal city.[160] Yemeni government forces also recaptured Jaar at almost the same time that they liberated Zinjibar, following a night evacuation of Ansar al-Shariah fighters from that city.[161] Government forces reported that they had captured an AQAP ammunition factory in Jaar, and killed more than 50 insurgent fighters in the area.[162] On June 12, Major General Salem Qatan, commander of the 31st Armored Brigade, announced that, "[t]he cities of Zinjibar and Jaar have been completely cleansed."[163] He made this announcement from the local government headquarters in Zinjibar. On June 14, Yemeni Defense Minister Mohammed Nasser Ahmed toured Zinjibar to demonstrate his safety in doing so and thereby underscore the government's control of the city.¹⁶⁴ Sadly, 6 days after he had made his announcement on liberating Zinjibar, General Qatan was killed by a suicide bomber in Aden, after the attacker ran up to his car behaving as a beggar seeking charity.¹⁶⁵

Yemeni government determination continued to produce results after the liberation of Zinjibar, which was widely viewed as a turning point in the struggle. In mid-June 2012, Yemeni army and militia forces captured the port town of Shaqra, the last major Ansar al-Shariah stronghold in Abyan province.¹⁶⁶ As the offensive pushed forward in late June 2012, Yemeni forces captured Azzan in Shabwa province, the last town held by Ansar al-Shariah in the southern and eastern provinces.¹⁶⁷ Yemeni Defense Ministry officials claimed to have captured a large cache of bombs and explosives in Azzan.¹⁶⁸ Many Yemenis were deeply surprised that the government had been able to retake captured territory so rapidly. Yemeni Brigadier General Mohammed al-Sawmali stated, "This is the end of al-Qaeda's aspirations to establish an Islamic rule in the south. There is no comeback to this."¹⁶⁹ General al-Sawmali also stated that he expected AQAP to continue to wage war against the government, with "selective operations targeting key political and military figures."¹⁷⁰ This prediction was later proven to be accurate. Also, in a last act of brutality before leaving civilian areas they had occupied, retreating Ansar al-Shariah forces planted mines throughout the area they were evacuating. On June 27, the Saudi press cited Yemeni officials as stating that 73 civilians had been killed by mines emplaced by the retreating insurgents.¹⁷¹ Three days later, that number rose to 81, although Yemeni military officials also claimed their forces had removed 3,000 landmines from the afflicted areas.¹⁷²

While a significant number of insurgents were killed in these battles, it was uncertain how many fighters had escaped to continue their armed struggle at a later time under more favorable circumstances. In Shabwa province, some tribal leaders were reported to be making an effort to persuade some of the defeated Islamist fighters to surrender and renounce their past affiliation with the militants. In Yemen, such leaders will sometimes guarantee the future good behavior of their tribal members in exchange for some sort of amnesty.[173] Unfortunately, these efforts do not seem to have produced significant results. AQAP may have been driven from the urban areas it had previously captured, but many of its members remained committed to the struggle.

In the aftermath of these defeats and the loss of territory, AQAP leaders continued to believe that they needed to assert the power and relevance of their organization and underscore their willingness to continue the struggle. Unsurprisingly, they fell back upon terrorism including a ferocious campaign of urban bombings and assassinations. On June 18, an AQAP suicide bomber killed Major General Salem Qatan in circumstances described earlier.[174] Another important assassination occurred on July 19, when Colonel Abdullah al-Maouzaei triggered a booby trap in his car in southern Yemen.[175] A less successful assassination attempt occurred in late July when an improvised explosive device (IED) attack wounded Air Force Colonel Yahia al-Rusaishan, but failed to kill him.[176] Al-Rusaishan had played an important role in hunting down AQAP members and survived three previous assassination attempts. The government responded to these attacks with intense investigations and claimed to have broken up a number of terrorist cells as a result.[177]

More spectacularly, in mid-July, an AQAP suicide bomber exploded himself outside of a police academy in Sanaa just as the police cadets were leaving the grounds. Twenty-two people, most of whom were cadets, were killed in the attack.[178] Security forces later arrested an individual whom they claimed helped plan the earlier suicide attack of the parade rehearsal and may well have been involved with the police academy bombing.[179] Outside of Sanaa, AQAP again undertook a major operation in which a suicide bomber killed 45 members of the Popular Defense Committee in Jaar. The leader of this unit, Abdul Latif al-Sayed, was among the dead, and dozens of other tribal fighters were wounded in the strike.[180] Another especially bold attack occurred in mid-August when AQAP terrorists killed 14 Yemeni soldiers in a grenade and car bomb attack on the intelligence service headquarters in Aden.[181]

Since that time, AQAP has remained active, and many other government security officials have been killed in bombings and drive-by shootings from cars or especially motorcycles.[182] AQAP leaders have stated that their operatives use motorcycles because they believe that they are less likely to be targeted by U.S. drones.[183] Intelligence and security officers were often favorite targets for assassination efforts, and officers of high rank known to be loyal to President Hadi were especially favored targets.[184] Leaders of political parties and government ministers were also frequent targets.[185] In this environment, Yemeni security forces have struck back hard and claim to have broken a number of AQAP terrorist plots before they were implemented.[186] According to government announcements, the security forces have arrested a number of aspiring suicide bombers who were planning attacks on government buildings, foreign embassies, military commanders, and other "important people."[187] In addition to their standard security activities, Yemeni officials initiated a strong crackdown against unlicensed motorcycles, especially in the south. While many of these measures may have been useful, AQAP remains a tough adversary capable of significant acts of domestic and international terrorism. They also remain interested in future political crises or breakdowns in Yemeni government authority that they may be able to exploit.

AQAP TERRORISM EFFORTS DIRECTED AGAINST THE UNITED STATES

During the 2009-12 time frame, AQAP continued to seek ways to strike against the United States, despite its focus on implementing the southern insurgency and waging the subsequent major battles in that region. AQAP leaders considered terrorist strikes against the United States and waging war against the Saleh government as overlapping priorities, despite the potential for a dissipation of resources with an overly ambitious agenda. There were some potentially high payoffs for such strategies despite the danger of overreach. A successful strike against the United States could vastly enhance AQAP's prestige as the cutting edge of jihadi terror, and thereby help to improve their recruiting and fundraising efforts. Moreover, AQAP leaders did not seem to fear a possible U.S. intervention with ground forces into Yemen in the aftermath of such a strike and may even have welcomed it. Had the United States invaded Yemen in response to a spectacular terror strike, it is almost certain that large elements of the population would have been willing to fight any foreign invader no matter how valid the reason for intervention might have been. In such circumstances, the U.S. leadership would have an overwhelming need to strike back hard and might easily choose the wrong way of doing so.

One of the first and most ambitious AQAP operations against the United States took place on December 25, 2009, when Umar Farouk Abdulmutallab, a Nigerian operative trained by AQAP in Yemen, attempted to blow up a Detroit-bound Northwest Airlines passenger jet that left Amsterdam, The Netherlands, with 280 people aboard. The failed terrorist was badly burned when a bomb sewn into his underwear did not detonate properly, and he was then handcuffed and restrained by airline personnel, so that he could be arrested when the aircraft landed. At his trial in the United States, Abdulmutallab pleaded guilty to eight charges related to the attack and called the bomb a "blessed weapon."[188] Abdulmutallab was found guilty and sentenced to life imprisonment. He also stated that he had met radical cleric Anwar al-Awlaki and been inspired by him to oppose the United States with violence.[189]

President Obama responded to the unsuccessful bombing attempt by announcing plans to expand efforts to help the Yemeni government implement an effective counterterrorism program. The President further maintained that he had "no intention of sending U.S. boots on the ground" to Yemen as a result of this incident, noting that, "in countries like Yemen, in countries like Somalia, I think working with international partners is most effective at this point."[190] President Obama's statement echoed earlier remarks by U.S. military leaders including Admiral Mike Mullen, then the Chairman of the Joint Chiefs of Staff, who asserted that sending U.S. combat troops to Yemen was "not a possibility."[191] In response to both the attempted terrorist strike and U.S. outrage, Yemen quickly announced that it had arrested 29 people believed to be members of AQAP in a domestic crackdown on that organization.

AQAP's next major operation against the United States involved parcel bombs sent by cargo aircraft from Yemen in October 2010, with the delivery firms United Parcel Service (UPS) and Federal Express. AQAP bombmakers had filled toner cartridges with explosive material and then had the explosives-laden parcels sent to the United States. According to journalistic sources, the attack failed when the packages were intercepted in London, UK, and Dubai, United Arab Emirates, as a result of information provided by Saudi intelligence.[192] The plan was apparently to have the packages detonate while the cargo aircraft were in flight and cause them to crash over the ocean. If this effort failed, the packages were addressed to be delivered to synagogues in the Chicago area where they would kill whoever opened them.

AQAP leaders have also been associated with efforts to incite Muslims in the West to strike against Western targets through the use of web-based technology.[193] In the past, internet jihadists have often been a limited threat. Many of these people enjoy placing blood curdling postings in internet chat rooms but balk at making any sort of serious sacrifice for radical causes. A few are more willing to play a serious role in jihad if they are properly recruited. AQAP has been willing to commit time and resources to overcome the problem of discerning potential recruits from bored hobbyists and recruited some deeply committed individuals to engage in acts of terrorism. Cell phone videos of al-Qaeda units fighting in Iraq have been reported to be an important tool for al-Qaeda recruitment efforts in Yemen.[194] The effort to identify and develop jihadists from the vast pool of internet radicals is difficult and time-consuming. Some problems of ineptitude can surface when using terrorists recruited over the Internet. Additionally, a variety of political changes in the Middle East may have influenced the climate and complicated efforts to recruit terrorists over the Internet. The U.S. withdrawal from Iraq, and the projected withdrawal from Afghanistan, seems to have reduced levels of anger in the Muslim world that AQAP recruiters have previously been able to exploit.

One AQAP leader who was widely suspected of inciting radicals and recruiting terrorists over the Internet is the now-deceased cleric, Anwar al-Awlaki.[195] U.S. Federal prosecutors in the first underwear bomber case believe Awlaki was directly involved in planning this attack.[196] He is also widely believed to have inspired and helped to radicalize a U.S. Army psychiatrist, who at this time is being prosecuted for an August 2009 shooting attack at Fort Hood, TX, where 13 people were killed and 32 wounded.[197] The psychiatrist is expected to plead innocent to the charges, although the basis for his defense is not yet clear. According to *Newsweek*, President Obama saw Awlaki as an exceptional danger, and told his advisors that Awlaki was an even higher priority for elimination or capture than Ayman al-Zawahiri, the leader of al-Qaeda following bin Laden's death.[198] This decision was not arbitrary. If Awlaki was the mastermind behind the first underwear bomber as federal prosecutors allege, his plan came quite close to killing 280 people, and perhaps even creating a situation where the U.S. leadership would be seriously pressured by domestic public opinion to invade Yemen. Such an invasion would produce an inflamed backlash among Yemen's tribes, who might then swell the ranks of AQAP. Under these circumstances, it is difficult to imagine such a war leading to a good outcome for the United States. U.S. forces could defeat Yemeni tribesmen on a consistent basis, but it is hard to see how they could transform Yemeni society in ways that would leave that country an ally following an eventual U.S. military withdrawal.

The U.S. emphasis on finding Awlaki produced results. The AQAP radical was killed on September 30, 2011, in the Yemeni town of Khashef by what the press describes as a Predator drone operated by the Central Intelligence Agency.[199] In his announcement on Awlaki's death, President Obama called his elimination a "major blow" in the struggle against al-Qaeda but gave almost no details about U.S. involvement in the operation. The U.S. Government has never acknowledged that a drone strike took place in this instance, and the Yemeni government also attempted to take credit for Awlaki's death in announcements to its own public.[200] In making this choice, President Obama was clearly aware of the inflammatory potential of a U.S. leader claiming to target and kill a terrorist suspect with a drone in Yemen in contrast to the Yemeni government's wishes. He therefore chose not to reveal any details that might embarrass that government.

The death of Anwar al-Awlaki has sometimes been identified as reducing the chances of further AQAP attacks against the United States, since websites associated with him advocated such strikes.[201] Unfortunately, this conclusion is an oversimplification which U.S. leaders need to avoid. AQAP clearly focused on Yemeni issues in 2011-12 due to the collapse of the

Saleh regime and the political turmoil surrounding this event, but international terrorism remained an important component of the organization's agenda. They have also indicated that victory in Yemen is considered a first step to a new campaign to overthrow the royal family in Saudi Arabia. Moreover, any doubts about AQAP's plans to continue efforts to attack Western targets were quickly set aside as a new AQAP plot against the United States was uncovered.

This 2012 plot centered on an effort to once again attack a U.S. airliner, this time with a modified and improved underwear bomb. According to the *Wall Street Journal*, the planned operation was efficiently uncovered as the result of the actions of a Saudi agent who had previously infiltrated AQAP and "volunteered" for a suicide mission in the knowledge that he would later be able to expose operational terrorist plans to the Saudi government.[202] The agent's superiors within AQAP accepted his offer and provided him with explosives, which were then turned over to Saudi intelligence. Information surrounding this incident was then shared with the United States. The plot did not appear to have moved forward, since the device was not seized at an airport and the mission had apparently not been assigned to a specific flight, according to the *Washington Post*.[203] U.S. officials have described the bomb used in this incident as an upgraded version of the 2009 device, but declined to give further details.[204] Yemeni officials and intelligence organizations appeared to have no knowledge of the plot.[205]

One particularly dangerous AQAP member who was reported to be involved with the ongoing efforts against the United States is Ibrahim Hassan al-Asiri. Asiri is a Saudi Arabian radical and bombmaker, who appears totally committed to opposing the Saudi monarchy and its allies. He has been credited with constructing both the first underwear bomb and the devices within the printer cartridges that were to be used for the parcel bombs.[206] He is also likely to have been responsible for the upgraded underwear bomb. Underscoring his commitment to AQAP, Asiri sent his own brother on an August 2009 mission to serve as a human bomb assigned to assassinate then Saudi Deputy Interior Minister and Chief of Counterterrorism, Prince Mohammed bin Nayef. Prince Mohammed led Saudi Arabia's campaign against domestic al-Qaeda supporters from 2003-12, and he was therefore an extremely important AQAP target both for operational reasons and for revenge. Asiri's brother had contacted the Prince with an offer to surrender and bring his supporters with him into the Saudi rehabilitation program. This plot failed when the energy of the human bomb was directed in unexpected ways and killed only the terrorist attacker. Prince Mohammad was only slightly hurt, although he undoubtedly emerged from the incident with a newfound caution regarding the enemy he was fighting. Prince Mohammad's effectiveness and his contribution to the struggle against AQAP were later recognized when he was appointed Saudi Arabian interior minister in November 2012.[207]

AQAP has also attacked U.S. and Western targets within Yemen, including the U.S. embassy, which was fired upon by mortar shells in March 2008. In this instance, the shells fell short of the embassy but killed a guard and injured 13 students at a nearby girl's school.[208] Two al-Qaeda members were later apprehended and sentenced to death for this action.[209] A larger and much better planned attack occurred on September 16, 2008, when six AQAP operatives disguised as police officers attacked the embassy with car bombs, killing 16 people including one American. Another serious attack against the Western diplomatic presence in Yemen occurred in April 2010 when an al-Qaeda suicide bomber attempted to kill the British ambassador by targeting his car convoy in Sanaa. The ambassador was unhurt, although three bystanders were wounded and the bomber killed.[210] The attempted assassination of a well-protected British diplomat was an embarrassment for the Yemeni government but not a crisis since no UK nationals were seriously injured or killed. More recently, in December 2012, three kilograms of gold (approximately U.S.$160,000) was offered for killing U.S. ambassador to Yemen Gerald Feierstein.[211] They also offered 5 million Yemeni riyals (U.S.$23,000) for the killing of any U.S. Soldier in Yemen.[212]

THE ISSUE OF DRONES

In addition to U.S. military assistance to Yemen, there is also a program to help the Yemenis with unmanned aerial vehicles (UAVs), often simply known as drones. The U.S. and world press often maintain that the Yemeni government victories in the 2012 offensive were greatly abetted, if not enabled, by the U.S. drone program put into place to support Yemeni ground forces. This is a difficult claim to assess, due to the lack of publically available details about the use of drones. Until recently, the U.S. leadership has been reluctant to admit any use of such systems in Yemen out of deference to sensitivities particularly apparent under President Saleh's leadership. Over time, however, this policy was relaxed due to the extensive U.S. and global media coverage of drone use, and the implausibility of further denials. In late April 2012, White

House Counterterrorism Adviser John O. Brennan stated publicly that the United States was using drone aircraft to strike against terrorism suspects and to prevent terrorist attacks on the United States, although he did not explicitly mention Yemen as a venue for such activities.[213] On October 11, 2012, U.S. Secretary of Defense Leon Panetta went further, noting that such systems have played a "vital role" in government victories over AQAP in Yemen, but did not elaborate further.[214] In a particularly forthcoming statement, Yemeni Foreign Minister Abu Bakr al-Qirbi told a reporter on the sidelines of a June 2012 counter-piracy conference in Dubai that, "drones were used upon Yemen's request against fleeing al Qaeda leaders" during the 2012 offensive.[215] Foreign Minister Qirbi's statement came in a context of the greater American openness about the use of these systems.

All remaining Yemeni government secrecy or deniability about drone use ended in September 2012 when President Hadi commented directly and extensively on the use of such systems. Hadi stated that he had allowed U.S. use of drones in Yemen to strike at terrorist targets. In doing so, he seems to have decided that there was no point in continuing Saleh's policy of denying drone strikes in Yemen since the strikes were routinely covered in the press, and virtually no one believed the government. Consequently, on a visit to the United States, Hadi informed the *Washington Post* that Yemen did allow U.S. drone strikes, but it also carefully regulated such activities.[216] According to the Yemeni president, U.S. drone attacks on Yemeni targets are not allowed unless he first approves them. Hadi has therefore taken responsibility for the strikes, while asserting that he does not allow the interests of the United States to supersede Yemeni interests. If a drone strike is not in the interests of Yemen, he refuses to authorize it. Moreover, Hadi also maintains that using drones helps ensure that only proper targets are hit and collateral damage is minimized. According to Hadi, "[t]he drone technologically is more advanced than the human brain," suggesting that these systems are more accurate than manned combat aircraft.[217] He also stated that Yemen's air force could not bomb accurately at night, but the U.S. drones did not have any problems in doing so. Hadi thereby asserted that the drones were a better system for avoiding mistakes and collateral damage. Also, in another very candid admission, Hadi acknowledged that some drone strikes have accidentally killed innocent people, but he also claimed that Yemen and the United States have taken "multiple measures to avoid mistakes of the past."[218]

Hadi's decision to acknowledge the U.S. use of drones in the struggle against AQAP drew a mixed response in Yemen. Some Yemenis appeared to appreciate that he was more open than Saleh and saw his honesty as a break from the past.[219] While drone strikes remain highly controversial in Yemen, the Yemeni public also seems to have become somewhat more tolerant of U.S. drone use over the last year than it was over earlier incidents. This change may be because the internal situation became more alarming, due to the rise of Ansar al-Shariah and the ability of these forces to take and hold a number of Yemeni towns and small cities throughout the Abyan and Shabwa provinces. Yet, even Yemenis who detest AQAP have been quick to maintain that innocent people have been accidentally killed by drones and that, at the very least, "tough limitations" must be imposed on such systems if they are to be used.[220] This situation will be difficult for the United States, since any serious mistake regarding collateral damage from drones could produce a domestic backlash which Yemeni politicians would be reluctant to ignore.[221] Moreover, a variety of powerful Yemeni politicians, including the radical Sunni cleric Abdul-Majeed al-Zindani, have sharply criticized the use of drones in Yemen and stand ready to take political advantage from any future incidents of collateral damage.[222] Such politicians will almost certainly exaggerate the number of innocents killed in strikes that involve civilian deaths.

The military value of the drone strikes is difficult to gauge, although the U.S. and international press have published vast numbers of articles on individual strikes with drone launched Hellfire missiles. It is not surprising that the press would latch on to such drama, but drones do more than simply serve as missile platforms. They also can serve as key intelligence platforms by virtue of their ability to linger over the battlefield and other areas of intelligence interest. This capability suggests that the drones are an important enabler of the efficient use of ground forces as well as missile platforms. In an offensive mode, drones were also an asset for killing militants preparing to attack Yemeni military forces at checkpoints or in the course of a battle. According to Yemeni news reports cited by the *New York Times*, some militants were killed by drones very shortly before they would have undertaken operations against government forces, including a few that were later found dead wearing suicide vests.[223]

One of the most important drawbacks of drones is their limited value as a strike weapon in circumstances where adequate intelligence about activities on the ground is not available. In Yemen, it can sometimes be difficult to discern AQAP operatives from other individuals simply on the basis of overflights. This issue is particularly problematic, since many Yemeni civilians who have nothing to do with AQAP are armed, and some tribal forces even have access to crew-served weapons, including machine guns and mortars. The obvious way to address this problem is through reliable intelligence which allows the drone operator to discern which targets are innocent and which are AQAP-affiliated. Nevertheless, intelligence is not always conclusive, and mistakes can be made. Gregory Johnsen, a leading scholar on Yemen, is particularly critical of drone use on these and other grounds. According to Johnsen, U.S. forces employing drones were excessively reliant on information provided by the Yemeni government under President Saleh, and this information was not trustworthy.[224] Johnsen also maintains that significant numbers of Yemenis have been radicalized by drone strikes that have killed innocent civilians on the basis of faulty intelligence.[225] This problem is particularly serious with Yemenis who have lost relatives in such strikes.

On balance, it appears that U.S. drone strikes in Yemen are not going to stop in the foreseeable future. While President Hadi and other Yemeni leaders may have to accept the political heat for allowing such strikes and deal with claims of collateral damage, this may not be the most serious political problem that they could have to address. A problem that would be even more serious is an inadequate response to AQAP's extensive assassination and bombing campaign. While terrorism is usually not as grave a problem as an expanding insurgency, it is still a severe threat, which has claimed the lives of a large number of Yemenis, and could again expand to the level of an insurgency. The greatest value of drones may be that they can help the United States achieve a satisfactory strategic outcome in Yemen and avoid factors that might lead to a wider U.S. involvement in a Yemeni war. Additionally, while drone use has many political drawbacks, the possibility that it helped determine the outcome of the summer offensive is worth considering. If the Yemeni military had been defeated by AQAP in this effort, the government might have collapsed at an excruciatingly sensitive time, possibly leaving the country in anarchy. Such a defeat would also have created the conditions for an even more deeply rooted AQAP presence in southern Yemen, with no countervailing Yemeni authority capable of moving against it. If Yemeni forces had failed, and particularly if they had failed ignominiously, a newly energized terrorist movement could have plagued the region and the world.

THE STRUGGLE TO REFORM THE YEMENI MILITARY AND THE ROLE OF U.S. MILITARY ASSISTANCE

The Yemeni military is in need of fundamental reform if it is to become an effective force for guaranteeing Yemeni sovereignty and maintaining the stability of the country against AQAP and other radical organizations. Earlier in this work, the success of the Yemeni military in the spring 2012 offensive against AQAP was noted. Driving AQAP from various contested southern provinces was an important victory, but it was not the last word on Yemeni military effectiveness, since the military did not achieve this victory alone. Yemeni military forces depended heavily on hired tribal units and, according to the international press, also especially depended on U.S. airpower, including drones.[226] The use of U.S. drones to ensure Yemeni security has already been seen to be unpopular among many Yemeni citizens and, under these circumstances, cannot be treated as a long-term solution to that country's security problems. Moreover, while AQAP was driven from captured territory in the 2012 offensive, it remains a powerful force capable of a wide range of aggressive actions against the Yemeni government and its people. Military reform therefore remains a vital aspect of dealing with Yemen's security problems.

As part of the GCC plan for Yemeni transformation under which President Hadi came to power, a military committee was established and given the task of managing and reducing tensions within the military created by the effort to oust President Saleh. At that time, military forces had become seriously divided between pro-Saleh and anti-Saleh factions led by Brigadier General Ahmed Saleh and Major General Ali Mohsen, respectively. These factions viewed each other as enemies during the last year of the Saleh presidency and became involved in occasional firefights on the streets of Yemeni cities. Clearly, the legacy of such confrontations produced deep and painful divisions in the military that would make it difficult to reestablish a united force.

While still vice president, Hadi formed a 14-member military commission to help oversee the reform and restructuring of the military and security forces, with the goal of limiting factionalism and centralizing presidential control of the military.[227] During his inaugural speech in February, the new president stated that his two top priorities were restructuring the armed forces, and launching a national dialogue among Yemeni civilian political factions. Many Yemenis seem to believe that military restructuring centers on removing the former president's relatives from important military posts, and little else is needed. Removing any untrustworthy officers is, of course, vital, but reform cannot stop there. A more reasonable end state for a reformed Yemeni military would be a well-equipped capable force that is able to minimize factionalism to the point that different units can work together effectively, and where competence trumps personal connections for promotions and key assignments. It is also important to reduce corruption within the armed forces, and ensure that lower ranking troops are paid their full salaries in a timely way to avoid the need for them to seek petty bribes while undertaking duties that place them in contact with the Yemeni public (such as manning military checkpoints).

Most serious observers of the Yemeni military have pointed out that throughout recent history each of the Yemeni brigades has acted more like an independent regionally-based militia loyal to its commander, rather than a force loyal to the national government.[228] Such an observation is hardly surprising since the salaries of Yemeni troops are sent to them from Sanaa through their local commanders. If they are paid promptly with minimal skimming, service members are particularly likely to view their regional commanders as the central focus of their loyalty. Moreover, a number of commanders report the presence of "ghost soldiers" on their rosters. These service members do not actually exist, but are paid monthly salaries that are pocketed by senior brigade officers.[229] This system of warlord-style military units is an important target for restructuring. Reformers suggest that Yemen needs to break away from this type of system in favor of a unified army that safeguards national stability and security and thereby boosts the Yemeni economy by attracting sorely needed foreign aid, investment, and tourism. If a centralized pay system that bypasses local commanders is possible, it could help ensure the loyalty of these troops to the larger nation and prevent them from being victimized by predatory officers.

Many Saleh loyalists remained in the military following their patron's departure from the presidency, but their numbers and influence have strongly diminished over time, with a series of reorganization measures taken by the new government. One of the first officers that President Hadi removed from command was General Mohammed Saleh, a half-brother of the former president and commander of Yemen's air force for over 20 years. At the time of Hadi's assumption of office, thousands of air force officers and airmen had been on strike for more than 2 months, closing down a number of air bases in at least four provinces.[230] The central demand of the rebellious forces was to have their commander removed. Air support for besieged forces in southern Yemen became problematic, and the general atmosphere of disorder within the military became more pronounced. In March 2012, the air force commander had pledged to relinquish this position in response to Hadi's orders, but he showed little movement toward doing so. It was also important to remove him quickly, and the foot dragging created military problems in pursing the struggle against AQAP.

General Mohammad Saleh was particularly detested for his leadership of the air force because many of his subordinates believed that he was skimming especially large amounts of money from funds designated to pay them, and was consequently responsible for the serious disruption of their pay.[231] In a familiar pattern, General Saleh resisted political pressure to leave office despite his previous promises to do so. When President Hadi stopped waiting for his promised resignation and removed him from the position of air force commander, he reacted by ordering troops loyal to him to seize Sanaa's main airport and force it to close for a day.[232] After this act of pique and defiance, General Saleh then backed down from a further confrontation in the face of Hadi's continued determination and the threat of court marshal for refusing a lawful order.[233] Additionally, UN Special Envoy to Yemen Jamal Benomar seems to have made an effort to convince both former President Saleh and his half brother to end this challenge to Hadi's authority in order to avoid sanctions directed at them personally.[234] The mutiny ended when General Saleh left his position to become a high ranking but powerless aide to the defense minister.[235]

Some of the more deeply entrenched Saleh loyalists took longer to remove from key positions of power. Former President Saleh's son, Ahmed, retained command of the elite Republican Guard, until December 2012, when he was scheduled to lose his position as a result of a planned merger of the Guard units into other forces within the Defense Ministry. Hadi almost certainly was uncomfortable to have Ahmed retain this position for so long, but may also have been concerned that immediately relieving him would introduce further divisions into the military at a point when they could least afford them. Hadi, therefore, eased Brigadier General Saleh out of his position of power in stages beginning in August 2012. At that time, he ordered a military reorganization which allowed Ahmed Saleh to retain his position as Republican Guard commander but seriously reduced the size and capabilities of the forces under his control.[236] This was done by transferring three brigades of the Republican Guard to the newly formed Presidential Protective Forces. The president also took some forces from units loyal to General Ali Mohsen al-Amar in an apparent effort to show at least a little balance by drawing forces from commanders hostile to each other.[237]

The August move to reassign personnel from the Republican Guard to Hadi's direct control infuriated many of Ahmed Saleh's supporters within that organization. Hundreds of Republican Guard members loyal to him surrounded the Defense Ministry shortly after the military reorganization decree was made public. These troops fired rifles and rocket-propelled grenades at ministry guards, initiating a gun battle that resulted in the deaths of two facility guards, two civilians, and one attacker.[238] In the immediate aftermath of this battle, 62 officers and soldiers were charged with mutiny and resisting authority. Later additional arrests were made, and the number of individuals arrested for attacking the Defense Ministry rose to 130.[239] Hadi's forceful reaction to the mutineers met the need to maintain military discipline, but the entire incident underscored the problems inherent in making any decisive moves to engage in serious command restructuring. Ahmed Saleh was never publicly linked to the attack and was not charged for conspiracy, incitement, or any other offense related to it. Members of the Republican Guard who had been arrested in the incident were variously charged with a number of serious offenses. These included deserting military posts, refusing orders, murder, and attempted murder. Ninety-three guardsmen were convicted of offenses of some kind and given prison sentences of 3 to 7 years.[240] These sentences seemed remarkably light, considering the seriousness of the charges. Some of the guardsmen were also acquitted.

Friction between President Hadi and Ahmed Saleh erupted again in December 2012 over the custody of Yemen's SCUD missiles. Yemeni SCUDs have not been equipped with chemical or other unconventional warheads, and therefore serve only as a delivery system for a relatively small amount of high explosive ordinance. Despite these limitations, surface-to-surface ballistic missiles are clearly a prestige weapon, and Hadi's order for the Republican Guard to turn them over to the Defense Ministry was not well-received. Initially, General Saleh refused to carry out the order, and the disagreement between Hadi and Saleh was reported to be quite intense.[241] After several days of confrontation, the Republican Guard commander backed down and agreed to allow the Defense Ministry to take custody of the missiles. The SCUD forces were redesigned as the Missiles Group, which was considered a strategic reserve force.

The most serious blow to General Ahmed Saleh's standing was the previously noted abolition of the Republican Guard, announced in December 2012 shortly after the SCUD confrontation by President Hadi's office. Perhaps as something of a sweetener, General Ali Moshin's 1st Armored Brigade was also formally abolished and was slated to have its troops transferred into newly reorganized units. The abolition of the Republican Guard is an interesting and dramatic step, although it is not clear how this will actually occur or how long it will take. The head of Yemen's Military Study Center, Staff Brigadier Ali Naji Obaid, stated somewhat cryptically that, "The unit labels are done for, but the forces are still standing."[242] Also somewhat unexpectedly, Ahmed Saleh publicly accepted the decision to abolish the Republican Guard. This acceptance may have been an act of military professionalism, but it is also possible that he could seek to implement the reorganization order in ways that are slow, shallow, and reversible. Saleh remains a general, and it is also possible that he will be transferred to a regional unit away from the levers of power in Sanaa.[243]

Another important relative, former President Saleh's nephew, Brigadier General Yaya Mohammed Abdullah Saleh, was retained in office as the commander of the Central Security Services (CSS) but was demoted in May 2012, and then removed from the CSS entirely in December 2012.[244] Yaya was the commander of the CSS until the May 21 suicide bombing, after which he was unable to retain that position but was allowed to remain with his unit, serving as Chief of Staff and Deputy Commander. Previously, Yaya had stated that, as a professional soldier, he will always remain loyal to the Republic, which means supporting Hadi as the elected president. This stance is laudable, but it may not be totally without guile. Yaya is frequently rumored to be interested in running for president when Hadi's 2-year transitionary term expires in 2014. By stressing the need for respect of republican principles, he avoids antagonizing the opposition while not undermining potential backing from his uncle's supporters. Yaya continues to deny interest in running for the presidency, but speculation on this issue continues.[245]

Another Saleh nephew, Brigadier General Tareq Mohammed Abdullah Saleh, lost his position as the commander of the presidential guard immediately following Hadi's election. He was transferred to a position as commander of the 3rd Armored Brigade, but this was not an appointment that Hadi wanted to last for long. The 3rd Brigade is the most heavily armed force of the Republican Guard, with troops throughout Sanaa, and thus not a good place to assign an untrustworthy commander.[246] On April 6, 2012, Tareq Saleh was reassigned as commander of the 37th Armored Brigade in Hadramawt Province in southern Yemen.[247] This posting was a much less politically sensitive assignment, although it was much closer to areas then contested by AQAP.

President Hadi has also made incremental but significant efforts to restructure the leadership of the military in response to military setbacks in the insurgency war with AQAP. On March 2, 2012, for example, he appointed Major General Salem Ali Qatan to command the 31st Armored Brigade, replacing Saleh loyalist Major General Mahdi Maqola.[248] This was not a controversial move, since Maqola had been the commander of the southern region during the February 18 defeat by AQAP, and a number of his actions were subject to severe criticism.[249] Qatan, by contrast, went on to play a leading role in the offensive that drove AQAP from the territory it had captured the previous year, although he was later assassinated by AQAP.

The future role of General Ali Mohsin al-Ahmar remains in question. Although he changed sides and supported the demonstrators early in the Arab Spring uprising, Ali Mohsin was for decades a powerful symbol of the old regime. He has also been an exceptionally powerful officer in the past, although he has been careful not to appear interested in overshadowing President Hadi. Ali Mohsin's adept political maneuvering nevertheless did not save the most important element of his power base when, in December 2012, the 1st Armored Brigade was abolished along with the Republican Guard. As at least a quasi-ally of Hadi, Ali Mohsin may have a potential for a political comeback and may also have had some ability to protect his protégés within the military.

In addition to reducing military factionalism, Hadi has emphasized the need to improve the basic combat skills of the military. To achieve this goal, the president has strongly asserted that his country needs a great deal of military aid from partner nations and emphasized the need for this help on a number of occasions. Moreover, this aid does not simply involve funding. The Yemeni military also needs assistance in organization and training. The United States is one of a number of countries helping Yemen meet these military requirements. Hadi's government remains in continuing and detailed discussions with U.S. leaders on the nature of such aid.

As the importance of Yemen has become increasingly clear to the West, so has U.S. military assistance to that country. This aid had expanded from a modest $4.3 million in 2006 to $66.8 million in 2009,[250] then surged to $176 million in 2010, partially as a result of the failed 2009 Christmas Day terrorist strike. Some of these additional funds were used to purchase four *Huey II* (UH-1H) helicopters and a CN-235-300 M fixed wing transport aircraft.[251] U.S. aid then dropped to $30 million in 2011 as the aid relationship collapsed in March, and the delivery of the helicopters and transport aircraft was also frozen.[252]

Under both Saleh and Hadi, U.S. military aid was primarily used to upgrade and improve the weapons, equipment, and training of the Yemeni forces. A sizeable amount of the U.S. aid was also directed at elite counterterrorism units and aviation assets. To further support Yemen, President Obama significantly and publicly increased intelligence support for that country until the March 2011 massacre of civilian demonstrators by Saleh's security services.[253] After the March crisis, Saleh seemed to hope that his problems with the United States aid suspension would be temporary and that the aid relationship might be reestablished as a result of U.S.-Yemeni cooperation on some terrorism issues, including finding and eliminating terrorist leader Anwar al-Awlaki. Saleh also sent limited numbers of his elite troops to fight against AQAP in the south, but would not allow the transfer of too many of them due to the ongoing power struggle in Sanaa. In June 2011, a Yemeni government spokesman confirmed that U.S.-trained counterterrorism troops affiliated with the Central Security Forces had deployed against opposition tribesmen.[254]

President Saleh's resignation and Hadi's assumption of Yemen's presidency allowed the United States to restore direct assistance to the Yemeni military which was begun gradually, with a special emphasis on units involved in the fight against AQAP.[255] Hadi's willingness to conduct a military offensive to evict AQAP from its southern strongholds impressed the U.S. leadership, and suggested that the new president was committed to a strong partnership in fighting terrorism. The United States is particularly interested in helping the Counter Terrorism Unit (CTU) which has previously benefited from U.S. aid and training. The United States also remains interested in helping the Yemenis maintain and upgrade their military helicopters and fixed wing aircraft so that elite troops can be quickly transported to areas where they are needed.

Some support for rebuilding the Yemeni military has also been provided by friendly Arab countries. The GCC has provided extensive funding for military assistance, but the most active Arab participant in Yemeni issues has been Jordan. The Jordanians also have a long history of cooperating with Gulf Arab states in working against radical organizations, including al-Qaeda and its various branches. Jordan maintains one of the finest armies in the Arab world, and it also has excellent, although low-technology, intelligence services. The Amman leadership has shown considerable interest in sharing its national security expertise through continuing cooperation with the Yemenis against AQAP, which the Jordanians also regard as an enemy. Talks on anti-terrorist cooperation date back to the Saleh regime and have continued at high levels under Hadi.[256]

Jordan has been working with the United States to provide expertise in the restructuring of the Yemeni military, particularly the army, including providing recommendations of "best practices" for the military restructuring.[257] A Jordanian military committee has also been deeply involved in providing recommendations to the Yemeni Defense Ministry and the Interior Ministry. Yemeni General Riyadh al-Qirshi has stated that the Jordanian committee, "includes a broad range of security experts who specialize in reorganizing public sector and military systems."[258] Jordan has also offered to help retrain the Yemeni military and expand the military ties between the two countries. This cooperation includes counterterrorism training at the King Abdullah II Special Operations Training Center (KASOTC) which had already occurred on a limited basis dating back to the Saleh regime.[259] This center was designed with U.S. assistance to help improve the military skills of Arab students, including non-Jordanians attending courses there.[260] KASOTC became fully operational on May 20, 2009, in a ceremony presided over by the Jordanian king.[261] Jordanian programs to train Yemenis at this facility will also have the advantage of reducing or eliminating language and cultural problems between Yemenis and their trainers.

It is also possible that Yemeni military forces could benefit from increased combined exercises with other Arab states and even peacekeeping training. Again, the role of Jordan could be useful in teaching Yemen troops how to address some security problems, with minimum force being directed at the population in conflict areas. While the Jordanian approach to this issue specializes in international peacekeeping, some of the principles used in an international environment may be relevant to various trouble spots in southern Yemen. Jordan maintains a Peacekeeping Operations Center based in Zarqa. Statistics from 2010 indicate that 61,000 Jordanian troops have participated in peacekeeping operations in 18 conflict areas, and this mission remains ongoing.[262] Such experience gives the Jordanians a wealth of information that the Yemenis may find useful. Since Jordan is not a wealthy country, funding from the United States, the EU, wealthy Arab states, or elsewhere would be needed to move forward on such efforts.

CONCLUSION, IMPLICATIONS FOR LANDPOWER, AND RECOMMENDATIONS

The security problems in Yemen, including the continued threat of AQAP, will not be resolved easily and will require a serious commitment of resources by a number of concerned countries to be effective. Moreover, it is difficult to solve the AQAP problem in any fundamental way without corresponding progress in managing the other difficulties in Yemen. President Obama's statement that he has "no intention" of sending combat troops (beyond military advisors and trainers) to Yemen is reassuring to most Yemenis, and indicates reasonable concern over the danger of being drawn into a significant military intervention that will almost certainly create more problems than it solves. Such an intervention would consume U.S. lives and resources and could only make the security situation in the region increasingly unstable, due to an inevitable nationalist backlash. This set of problems does not suggest that the United States can remain aloof from Yemen's problems. Rather, it requires that Washington's involvement in Yemen must be structured in ways that the political culture will accept.

U.S. support for Yemen remains important, and the United States must not regard the fight against AQAP as largely over because of the defeat of their insurgent forces in the south. This analysis has shown that AQAP remains a dangerous and effective force despite these setbacks. There are also important reasons for defeating AQAP and its allies in Yemen, even if this does not destroy the organization and instead leads it to move operations to prospective sanctuaries in other remote parts of the world. Yemen is one of the worst places on earth to cede to terrorists due to its key strategic location, including a long border with Saudi Arabia. It also dominates one of the region's key waterways, the Bab al-Mandeb Strait which controls access to the southern Red Sea. Furthermore, the problem of Yemen based-terrorism remains an important international threat which cannot be ignored, as indicated by repeated AQAP efforts to attack the U.S. homeland.

Unfortunately, the Yemeni political system is likely to remain unstable, and the economic system is virtually certain to remain impoverished for some time. Central governmental authority in the hinterland can be expected to remain limited for the foreseeable future. Within this especially difficult milieu, this report makes the following recommendations:

1. The United States must strongly support the transitional government of President Hadi as long as he continues to stand firmly against AQAP, and as long as the Yemeni government adheres to a pro-reform agenda, including a firm commitment to a new democratic constitution. This effort will involve both military and civilian aid. Some segments of the Yemeni population are particularly suspicious that the United States cares nothing about Yemen except for the fight against AQAP. Superficially, that may appear to be the case, but U.S. military leaders have a more sophisticated understanding of the nature of counterinsurgency, including the fact that over time you cannot be better at counterinsurgency than the government you support. U.S. aid, including military aid, must therefore continue to be grounded in an understanding of Yemeni political culture, and the importance of reform.

2. The United States must not seek to Americanize the struggle against AQAP, and should avoid sending major ground combat units to Yemen. However bad the situation may become there, appearing to Americanize the war against AQAP can only make it dramatically worse. Yemeni public opposition to the presence of foreign ground troops with combat missions is almost universal, and it is possible that large elements of the Yemeni public would rise against their president and parliament if the government invited the United States to provide such forces. Certainly, Yemen's Islamic clergy can be particularly shrill on

this subject, and this intensity goes far beyond well-known radicals such as Sheikh Zindani.

3. U.S. leadership needs to avoid viewing the U.S. drone program as a panacea for terrorism and insurgency problems in Yemen. While this report does not recommend discontinuing drone use over Yemen, it does urge the U.S. leadership to consider drone use to be a limited term solution for efforts to deal with AQAP. The long-term solution must be a reformed Yemeni military that can address problems, such as AQAP, without the need for any direct U.S. military intervention, including the use of armed drones. In this regard, the nature and extent of the drone program anywhere in the world can provoke a strong local backlash. Correspondingly, drones cannot be viewed as a "cost-free" form of warfare despite their advantages. As previously noted, widespread journalistic coverage of the use of these systems in Yemen suggests a continuing high level of Yemeni public discontent about the program even if the discontent is currently manageable by the Yemeni government. It is also of tremendous importance that the United States avoid civilian casualties resulting from drone strikes to the greatest extent possible. This priority is not simply a humanitarian concern. The tribal nature of Yemen ensures that any civilian casualty will have a number of living relatives and fellow tribesmen who will never forgive such an assault. These people could be encouraged to join AQAP in direct response to the deaths of any innocents with whom they feel kinship.

4. U.S. policymakers should encourage the Yemeni government to continue supporting local anti-AQAP Resistance Councils, provided they share a similar

agenda to the government. Many southern Yemeni tribes and individuals continue to hold grudges against AQAP for the brutal ways in which they behaved in 2010-12 when they occupied and administered territory in key southern provinces. There also exists a strong secular trend, at least in the urban areas of the south, and nostalgia for the socialist system that existed before 1990. That regime, for all its many crimes and shortcomings, is remembered as providing for the poor and needy, albeit with extensive Soviet bloc aid that artificially kept the economy afloat. Southerners, correspondingly, are not likely to embrace AQAP ideology in large numbers unless it is their only alternative. Moreover, as in 2012, many southern tribesmen and villagers will continue to fight against AQAP as tribal auxiliaries provided that they do not view the government of Yemen as worse than AQAP.

5. It would be useful for the U.S. Army and Marine Corps to share both counterinsurgency and counterterrorism lessons learned in Iraq with the Yemeni military, through a variety of interactions. The use of the Iraqi Awakening Councils seems to parallel the development of the Yemeni Resistance Councils to the point that a good consideration of the problems and advantages of Iraq could help Yemenis understand how to best conduct their own operations. Some of the lessons of the Awakening Groups in Iraq might be applied to the tribal organizations in Yemen. U.S. Army officers familiar with the lessons of the Iraqi Awakening Groups might make particularly good advisors for the Yemeni military. One particularly important way that the United States could help Yemen is to give them advice about vetting potential applicants for service in these organizations. Additionally, advice from

U.S. sources on comprehensive counterinsurgency efforts and strategies which go beyond simply defeating insurgents could be particularly valuable.[263] U.S. advisors might find it useful to emphasize how winning over the population can yield numerous military advantages such as an increased flow of high quality intelligence.

6. The United States should help Yemen rebuild its air force (including rotary and fixed-wing components) after the 2011-12 mutiny and other problems that it has experienced. In particular, the U.S. Army may be called upon to help train and support Yemeni use of assault and transport helicopters. Such systems are often exceptionally important for counterinsurgency. The Yemenis are also expected to receive additional transport aircraft such as C-130s. These systems are likely to be extremely useful in carrying troops, especially elite counterterrorism troops, as quickly as possible to places where they are needed. The Yemeni military should also be provided with militarily significant numbers of its own drones, even if these systems are not the most advanced systems available. The use of drones in Yemen is much more acceptable to the population if these drones are Yemeni rather than U.S. assets.

7. U.S. policymakers must continue supporting Yemeni government efforts to fight AQAP with intelligence, training, and military equipment, so long as Yemeni leaders continue to display a willingness to carry on the fight. So far, the United States has been highly effective in tailoring its military aid to Yemen in ways that focus on the needs of the counter al-Qaeda mission. Should AQAP be able to reestablish itself

as a powerful insurgent force, the United States will have to expand aid in ways that remain oriented on counterinsurgency. The United States will then have to do everything possible to avoid becoming viewed as a party to Yemen's other conflicts, such as the periodic fighting between the Yemeni government and the Houthi rebels in the north.

8. The United States must structure its military support to Yemen in ways that continue to support a long-term military relationship between the two countries, but that also expose the Yemenis to U.S. concepts of military professionalism. Such an approach would include particular vigilance in providing ongoing opportunities for Yemeni officers to train in the United States in programs such as Professional Military Education (PME) courses. Such courses give international officers an opportunity to forge close relationships with American officers and to consider the importance of respect for human rights within a military context.

9. U.S. leaders must be aware of the serious and escalating possibility of a humanitarian crisis occurring in Yemen. They must also seek ways to address this crisis without deploying large numbers of U.S. Army or Marine forces, if this is at all possible. If U.S. military forces must be deployed, efforts must be made to project as light a footprint as possible. Moreover, any U.S. organizations involved in humanitarian relief need to be aware that weak government institutions and endemic corruption will make it difficult to work with the government to implement a meaningful and efficient aid program.

10. The expansion of good governance and anti-corruption measures in Yemen is vital to that country's future, and any U.S. efforts to encourage and support these efforts may be useful. The United States has not been able to halt the rampant corruption in Afghanistan, Iraq, and Pakistan, and it cannot be expected to implement fundamental changes in Yemen. Nevertheless, ways need to be found to reduce corruption to the point that the intentions of important international aid projects are not subverted, and military forces do not have their efficiency undermined by corrupt practices.

11. The United States should support the work of effective and trustworthy nongovernmental organizations (NGOs) in Yemen. The United States cannot solve the problem of AQAP operations in Yemen with development aid administered by U.S. personnel, but it can certainly encourage and support the work of responsible NGOs and ask other developed countries to do the same. Their role is vital, since there are relatively few individuals in the Yemeni government who can impartially administer well-funded development programs. Such programs will have to address a myriad of economic problems in order to help Yemen in any meaningful way. Programs to help address the severe and rising problem of unemployment, particularly among young people, may be especially important. The Yemeni bureaucracy is not up to many of the tasks associated with development, since it is both riddled with internal problems and maintains only a limited ability to operate outside of Sanaa. This situation greatly magnifies the importance of NGOs.

12. As in Iraq and Afghanistan, the United States will have to be tolerant of the Yemeni government's willingness to pardon and rehabilitate former mem-

bers of AQAP who have not been involved in international terrorism and show good prospects for remaining outside of terrorist groups in the future. The Yemeni government also has to be careful about who it accepts into military service and service in the popular committees. Since many Yemeni fighters join radical organizations for pay rather than ideology, these people could stop being a problem if their energies can be directed elsewhere. Nevertheless, true radicals could also attempt to infiltrate Yemeni security organizations, and Yemeni leaders must guard against this danger.

ENDNOTES

1. Presidential Letter—2012 War Powers Resolution 6-month Report, Washington, DC: The White House, June 15, 2012.

2. John O. Brennan, "U.S. Policy Toward Yemen," New York: U.S. Council on Foreign Relations, August 6, 2012. Note: This presentation was given while Brennan was the Assistant to the President for Homeland Security and Counterterrorism.

3. "Yemeni President Vows Offensive against al Qaeda," *CNN.com*, May 5, 2012.

4. Saudi Arabia, with around 28 million people, technically has a larger population, although over five million of these people are non-nationals (including Yemenis) who have come to the country to work. If one subtracts non-nationals from the Saudi total, the two countries have almost equal populations at the present time.

5. Jeffery D. Feltman, Assistant Secretary, Bureau of Near Eastern Affairs, U.S. Department of State, and Robert F. Godec, Principal Deputy Coordinator for Counterterrorism, U.S. Department of State, "Yemen on the Brink: Implications of U.S. Policy: Statement before the House Committee on Foreign Affairs," State Department Press Release, Washington, DC: U.S. State Depart-

ment, February 3, 2010. Testimony on population included in this study is based on a U.S. Agency for International Development (USAID) funded study. Other sources have lower projections.

6. "GCC Meeting on Yemen," *Arab News*, March 21, 2012.

7. *Ibid*.

8. "UN Council concerned by new political troubles in Yemen," Agence Frances Presse, March 29, 2012.

9. Initially, Saleh was able to retain the presidency after the 1990 unification as a result of negotiations with southern politicians. Later he was elected to this post.

10. See April Longley Alley, "The Rules of the Game: Unpacking Patronage Politics in Yemen," *Middle East Journal*, Vol. 64, No. 3, Summer 2010, pp. 385-409.

11. *Ibid.;* see also Victoria Clark, *Yemen: Dancing on the Heads of Snakes*, New Haven, CT, and London, UK: Yale University Press, 2010, p. 191.

12. This type of system is discussed in Roger Owens, *The Rise and Fall of the Arab Presidents for Life*, Cambridge, MA: Harvard University Press, 2012.

13. Ahmed al-Haj, "Thousands Rally Against Government in Yemen," Associated Press, January 27, 2011; Sudarsan Raghavan, "In Yemen, Calls for Revolution But Many Hurdles," *The Washington Post*, January 31, 2011.

14. Laura Kasinof, "Yemen's Saleh Agrees Not to Run Again. Is That Good Enough for Protesters?" *Christian Science Monitor*, February 2, 2011.

15. Laura Kasinof, "Protesters Face Off for 7th Day in Yemen," *New York Times*, February 17, 2011.

16. Mohammed Ghobari and Khaled Abdullah, "Armed Yemen Loyalists Pursue Protesters," *Daily Star*, February 15, 2011. Also see "In Yemen's Tahrir Square, Pro-Government

Crowds Counter 'Day of Wrath'," *Christian Science Monitor*, February 3, 2011.

17. Laura Kasinof and Scott Shane, "Senior Yemeni Officers Call for Ouster of President," *New York Times*, March 22, 2011.

18. "Troops Blanket Sanaa after Yemen Declares Emergency," *Kuwait Times*, March 20, 2011.

19. "Top Army Commanders Defect in Yemen," *Al Jazeera.net*, March 21, 2011; Laura Kasinof, "Senior Yemeni Officers Back Protesters," *New York Times*, March 21, 2011.

20. "Hundreds" of troops of the Republican Guard were also reported to have defected to the protesters at the time, although this assertion remains difficult to verify and, in any event, was not the beginning of a trend. "Yemen Talks Make Some Headway," *Gulf Times*, November 21, 2011; Khaled al Hammadi, "Saleh's Death Grip Pulls Yemen's Army into Enemy Camps," *The National*, April 20, 2012.

21. The Saleh family currently regards Hamid al-Ahmar as an exceptionally dangerous foe who may seek to seize power if a reasonable opportunity presents itself to him. *Yemen: Enduring Conflicts, Threatened Transition*, Brussels, Belgium: International Crisis Group, 2012, p. 12.

22. "Emboldened Saleh Tells His Foes to Get Out," *Reuters*, March 30, 2011.

23. "Yemen's Saleh Stalling on Power Handover-Opposition," *Jordan Times*, November 19, 2011.

24. "Saleh Agrees to Step Down under GCC Deal," *Arab News*, April 24, 2011.

25. "Yemen's Saleh Defiant about Exit," *Reuters*, April 25, 2011.

26. Robert F. Worth, "President of Yemen Offers to Leave, With Conditions," *New York Times*, April 24, 2011.

27. Sudarsan Raghavan and Ali Almujahed, "Yemen Security Forces Kill Protesters," *The Washington Post*, April 4, 2011.

28. "Yemen Army Shells Southern City Killing 3; Anti-Government Protesters Converge for Rallies," *The Washington Post*, December 2, 2011; Mohammed Ghobari, "Yemeni Forces Fire on Protesters in South's Taiz," *Reuters*, July 28, 2011; "Yemeni Forces Kill 21 as Taiz Sit-In Smashed," *Kuwait Times*, May 31, 2011; Robert F. Worth, "Yemen on the Brink of Hell," *New York Times Magazine*, July 24, 2011.

29. "15 Dead as Yemen Truce Collapses Immediately," *Daily Star* (Beirut), October 26, 2011.

30. Mohammed al-Qadhi and Alice Fordham, "Fierce Fighting in Yemen as Political Talks Stall," *The Washington Post*, September 20, 2011.

31. "Conflicting Reports Emerge Over Saleh's Return," *Daily Star*, June 17, 2011.

32. "Fighting Erupts in Yemeni Capital, Six Killed," *Khaleej Times*, July 19, 2011.

33. Laura Kasinof, "Fighting Erupts for Second Day in Yemeni Capital," *New York Times*, September 19, 2011.

34. "Yemen's Saleh Makes Eid Plea for Peace," *Jordan Times*, November 7, 2011.

35. Mohammed Ghbari, "Yemen Vice President Says Power Handover Deal Close," *Reuters*, November 12, 2011; "EU to Discuss Sanctions on Yemen's Saleh," *Khaleej Times*, November 8, 2011.

36. Margaret Coker and Hakim Almasmari, "Leader Leaves Yemen, Bound for U.S.," *The Wall Street Journal*, January 23, 2012; "Yemen Scaps Amnesty for Saleh's Aides," *Khaleej Times*, January 21, 2012.

37. "Prolonging the Inevitable in Yemen," *Gulf Today*, January 21, 2012.

38. "Yemen Leader Has Reneged on Promises: Clinton," *Khaleej Times*, January 18, 2012.

39. "Yemen PM Says Interim Govt to be Put Up Soon," *Arab News*, December 7, 2011.

40. Sudarsan Raghavan, "Yemeni President Hands Over Power, But Little Changes," *The Washington Post*, December 3, 2011.

41. Ahmed al-Haj, "Yemen's Saleh Leaves for US, Says He Will Be Back," *The Christian Science Monitor*, January 22, 2012.

42. "Saleh En Route to US, Soldiers Want Air Force Chief Out," *Gulf Times*, January 24, 2012.

43. Nasser Arrabyee, "Without Saleh," *Al Ahram Weekly* (Egypt), April 20, 2012.

44. Ahmed al-Haj, "Yemen says More Than 2,000 Killed in Uprising," Associated Press, March 18, 2012.

45. Peter James Spielman, "Report: Yemen Killed 270 in Arab Spring Protest," Associated Press, February 8, 2012.

46. "65 Percent of Yemeni Voters Pick a New President," *Khaleej Times*, February 25, 2012; "2 Killed as Yemen Army Fires on Anti-Election Protesters," *Arab News*, February 10, 2012; "Yemen Separatists Urge Supporters to Disrupt Poll," *Gulf Times*, February 19, 2012.

47. "Yemen's Election," *The Economist*, February 25, 2012.

48. *Ibid.*

49. Mohamed Bin Sallam, "Yemen's President-in-Waiting," *Yemen Times*, February 19, 2012.

50. Mahmoud Habboush and Tom Finn, "Yemen's Hadi Emerges from Shadow to Lead Divided Country," *Reuters*, February 2012.

51. "Hadi Refused to Attend GPC Meetings," *Yemen Post*, April 15, 2012.

52. Ahmed al-Haj, "Official: Yemen leader Mulls Dismissing Government," Associated Press, March 20, 2012.

53. Sudarsan Raghavan, "In Yemen, Uncontested Presidential Vote on February 21 Masks Tension over Saleh's Successor," *The Washington Post*, February 14, 2012.

54. "Sources: Saleh Ordered Officials to Refuse Presidential Decrees," *Yemen Post*, April 10, 2012.

55. "Yemen Protesters Demand Ex-President Face Trial," *Khaleej Times*, March 24, 2012.

56. "Saudi King Orders Petroleum Aid to Yemen," Agence France-Presse, March 27, 2012.

57. "EU to Discuss Sanctions on Yemen's Saleh," *Khaleej Times*, November 8, 2011.

58. Associated Press, "Yemeni Officials Say Navy Shelling Has Killed 29 al-Qaida Militants in Southern Coastal Region," *The Washington Post*, March 22, 2012.

59. "Saleh Interfering in Transition: Minister," *Gulf Times*, September 23, 2012.

60. Karen DeYoung, "President Obama Executive Order Gives Treasury Authority to Freeze Yemeni Assets in U.S.," *The Washington Post*, May 15, 2012; Ken Dilanian and David S. Cloud, "A Deepening Role for the U.S. in Yemen," *Los Angeles Times*, May 17, 2012.

61. *Yemen: Enduring Conflicts, Threatened Transition*, p. 7.

62. Associated Press, "Leader of Yemen's al-Qaeda Branch Pledges Allegiance to bin Laden Successor al-Zawahiri," *The Washington Post*, July 26, 2011.

63. Brynjar Lia, *Architect of Global Jihad, The Life of Al-Qaida Strategist Abu Mus'ab al-Suri*, New York: Columbia University Press, 2008, p. 275.

64. Bruce Maddy-Weitzman, *Middle East Contemporary Survey*, Vol. XXI, Boulder, CO: Westview, 1997, p. 769.

65. Robert Lacey, *Inside the Kingdom*, New York: Viking, 2009, pp. 204-206.

66. Clark, p. 163.

67. *Ibid.*, p. 167.

68. Gregory D. Johnsen, "The Resiliency of Yemen's Aden-Abyan Islamic Army," *Jamestown Foundation Terrorism Monitor*, July 13, 2006; Michael Knights, "Internal Politics Complicate Counterterrorism in Yemen," *Jane's Intelligence Review*, February 1, 2006.

69. Clark, p. 223.

70. Gregory D. Johnsen, "AQAP in Yemen and the Christmas Day Terrorist Attack," *West Point Counter Terrorism Center Sentinel*, January 2010, p. 5; "Wolfowitz: U.S. Missile Strike Kills al Qaeda Chief," *CNN.com*, November 5, 2002.

71. Gregory D. Johnsen, "Al-Qaeda Makes a New Mark in Yemen," *Asia Times Online*, July 4, 2007.

72. *Ibid.*, p. 227.

73. Gordon Lubold, "New Look at Foreign Fighters in Iraq," *The Christian Science Monitor*, January 7, 2008.

74. Clark, p. 227.

75. See Ed Blanche, "An Al Qaeda Rolodex," *The Middle East*, March 2008, pp. 7-10; Clark, p. 203.

76. Michael Isikoff, "Deadly Training Ground," *Newsweek*, September 17, 2008, available from *www.newsweek.com*; "US Embassy Attacks Said Linked to Al-Qaeda," *The Washington Post*, November 2, 2008.

77. Norman Cigar, *Al Qa'ada's Doctrine for Insurgency*, Dulles, VA: Potomac Books, 2009, pp. 49-51.

78. "Yemen Frees 170 al-Qaeda Suspects," *Saudi Gazette*, February 9, 2009.

79. Joanna Sugden, "'Hundreds of al-Qaeda Militants Planning Attacks from Yemen,'" *Times* Online (*London Sunday Times*), December 29, 2009, available from *www.timesonline.co.uk*; Henry Meyer, "Al-Qaeda Claims Failed Attack on UK Envoy to Yemen, SITE Says," *Bloomberg.com*, May 12, 2010.

80. Sudarsan Raghavan, "In Yemen, U.S. Airstrikes Breed Anger, and Sympathy for al-Qaeda," *The Washington Post*, May 29, 2012.

81. "Al-Qaeda in Yemen on the Run as Military Regains Control over 2 of Its Strongholds," *The Washington Post*, June 12, 2012.

82. Christopher Swift, "To Defeat Al-Qaeda, Win in Yemen," *Bloomberg.com*, June 21, 2012.

83. On Pakistanis in Yemen, see "Yemen Says Town Free of Qaeda Grip," *Gulf Times*, August 25, 2010.

84. "Yemeni Troops, Qaeda Battle in Restive South, Clashes Leave 124 Dead in Yemen," *Kuwait Times*, April 11, 2002; Ahmed al-Haj, "Yemen: Fighting in South Kills 50 Militants," Associated Press, April 12, 2012.

85. "Al-Qaeda-Linked Group Gives Yemen Government Ultimatum," *Gulf Times*, March 1, 2012.

86. "Profile: Ansar al-Sharia in Yemen," *BBC News Online*, March 18, 2012; "Filling the Void-AQAP Attempts a Takeover in Yemen," *Jane's Intelligence Review*, December 16, 2011; Sudarsan Raghavan, "Militants Linked to al-Qaeda Emboldened in Yemen," *The Washington Post*, June 12, 2011.

87. Ignatius made this evaluation after being granted U.S. Government access to some of the documents captured in the raid in Abbottabad. See David Ignatius, "Bin Laden's Plot to Kill Obama," *The Washington Post*, March 18, 2012.

88. "Suicide Attack Kills Soldiers in Southern Yemen," *BBC News Online*, March 13, 2012.

89. "133 Killed as Yemen Forces Battle Qaeda," *Gulf Times*, April 11, 2012.

90. Lynne Nahhas, "Yemen FM Admits US Drones Used against Qaeda," Agence France-Presse, June 27, 2012.

91. "10 Die in Fresh Yemen Qaeda Battles," *Gulf Times*, April 13, 2012; "Yemen Officials Says Suspected US Drone Strikes Kill 11 Al-Qaida Fighters in Country's South," Associated Press, May 12, 2012.

92. "Al Qaeda Militants Take Control of Another Yemen Province," *The National*, March 13, 2012.

93. "Militants Free 73 Captured Yemen Troops," *Gulf Times*, April 30, 2012.

94. Ibid.

95. Gregory D. Johnsen, *The Last Refuge: Yemen, al-Qaeda, and America's War in Arabia*, New York: W. W. Norton & Company, 2013, pp. 57-58.

96. *The 9/11 Commission Report*, New York: W. W. Norton & Company, 2004, pp. 190-191.

97. Tabassum Zakaria and Mark Hosenball, "Why Bin Laden disapproved of Al Qaeda in Yemen, Iraq, and Somalia," *The Christian Science Monitor*, May 4, 2012.

98. AQIM, while often bumbling in its early years as a terrorist organization, has been able to generate funds through kidnapping for ransom, drug trafficking and other smuggling related ac-

tivities. See "Al-Qaeda 3.0: Exploiting Unrest from Syria to Sahel: Expert," Agence France-Presse, January 26, 2013;

99. Johnsen, *The Last Refuge*, p. 246.

100. Tahir Haydar, "Al Qaida Amir in Abyan: We Want Taliban Rule," *al-Ray Online* (Kuwait), February 6, 2012, (Arabic).

101. "Amnesty Slams Yemen Military, al Qaeda for Rights Abuse," *Reuters*, December 4, 2012.

102. Ahmed al-Haj and Aya Batrawy, "Amnesty Details 'Horrific' Abuses in South Yemen," Associated Press, December 4, 2012.

103. Andrew Hammond, "Wary Yemen Refugees Returning to Former Qaeda-Run Towns," *Reuters*, October 17, 2012.

104. "Yemen Says Town Free of Qaeda Grip"; "Obama's Other Surge—in Yemen," *The Christian Science Monitor*, August 25, 2010.

105. "Yemen Says Seven Qaeda Members Among 21 Killed in South," Agence France-Presse, August 21, 2010; "Yemen Army 'Regains Control' of Southern Town," Agence France-Presse, August 25, 2010.

106. Casualties were reported as in the "dozens," which is not high for urban combat involving significant numbers of troops. It is, however, possible that the government has minimized security forces casualties. See Agence France-Presse, "Thousands Protest 'Blockage' of South Yemen City Loder," *Daily Star*, September 17, 2010.

107. Fawaz al-Haidari, "10 Killed in Fresh Yemen Qaeda Battles," Agence France-Presse, April 12, 2012.

108. "32 Killed as Yemen Battles al-Qaeda for Key Town," *Daily Star*, April 11, 2012.

109. Robert F. Worth, "Yemen Military Attacks Town it Says is Militant Hide-out," *New York Times*, September 21, 2010.

110. "Thousands Flee Fighting in Yemen's Shabwa Province," *BBC News Online*, September 20, 2010.

111. "Al-Qaeda Militants Using Human Shields in Yemen Town—Official," *Jordan Times*, September 22, 2010.

112. "Three Police Killed in Yemen Attack," United Press International, August 26, 2010.

113. Nadia al-Sakkaf, "Al-Qaeda Steps Up Its Tactics as the Government Strikes Harder," *Yemen Times*, September 16, 2010; Robert F. Worth, "Yemen Military Besieges Remote Qaeda Redoubt," *New York Times*, September 21, 2010.

114. See, for example, "Yemeni Police Chief Shot Dead," *Gulf Today*, October 15, 2010.

115. Agence France-Presse, "Yemen Tribesmen to Stop Harboring Qaeda Suspects," *Daily Star*, June 14, 2010.

116. The exception to this principle would be where AQAP-aligned tribes have leaders who are also significant within AQAP.

117. Jeb Boone, "Yemen's Saleh Cedes al Qaeda Hotbed to Militants. Why?" *The Christian Science Monitor*, May 31, 2011.

118. Acil Tabbara, "'Al Qaeda' Seizure of Yemen City Raises Questions," *Jordan Times*, May 31, 2011.

119. *Ibid.*

120. Mohammed Mukhashaf, "Besieged South Yemen Brigade Appeals for Help," *Reuters*, July 3, 2011.

121. "Yemen Warplanes Bomb South, 8 Die," *Kuwait Times*, July 6, 2011.

122. "Al 'Qaeda' Suicide Bomber Kills 9 Yemeni Troops," *Jordan Times*, July 25, 2011.

123. "Yemeni Army Shelling Kills More than 20 Militants," *Khaleej Times*, July 20, 2011; "Yemen Army Shells Qaeda Posts, Kills 12," *Khaleej Times*, February 15, 2012.

124. Laura Kasinof, "Strategic Site Is Captured by Militants in Yemen," *New York Times*, June 29, 2011.

125. Sudarsan Raghavan, "'We Are Like an Island in a Sea of al-Qaeda,'" *The Washington Post,* January 1, 2012.

126. "Planning to Attack the Vital Security and Oil Installations as Well as Al-Mullaks Port," *Akhbar al-Yom* Online, March 7, 2012, (Arabic).

127. "Al-Qaeda Militants Tighten Grip on Yemeni Town," *Arab News*, January 17, 2012.

128. Agence France-Presse, "Al Qaeda Overruns Town Near Yemen Capital," *Jordan Times*, January 17, 2012.

129. Damien McElroy, "Drone Attacks Surge on Terror Targets in Yemen," *Sydney Morning Herald*, March 30, 2012.

130. "Deadly Blast Overshadows Yemen Power Transition," *Gulf Times*, February 26, 2012; Laura Kasinof, "Yemen Swears in New President to the Sound of Applause, and Violence," *New York Times*, February 25, 2012.

131. Kasinof, "Yemen Swears in New President to the Sound of Applause, and Violence."

132. "Filling the Void—AQAP Attempts a Takeover in Yemen," *Jane's Intelligence Review*, December 16, 2011.

133. Mohammed al-Kibsi, "Al-Qaeda Clashes Yemen Army in Two Towns," *Yemen Observer*, September 15, 2011.

134. "Suspected US Drone Kills Two Yemeni al Qaeda Men," *Jordan Times*, May 6, 2012.

135. Fawaz al-Haidari, "Yemen Army Death Toll from Qaeda Assault Jumps to 185," Agence France-Presse, March 6, 2012.

136. "Yemen Army Death Toll from al Qaeda Assault Jumps to 185," *Jordan Times*, March 7, 2012.

137. "Yemen President Vows to Pursue al-Qaeda-Linked Militants," *Jordan Times*, March 6, 2012.

138. Ahmed Dawood, "Yemen's Counter-Terrorism Unit to Fight Ansar al-Sharia," *Yemen Times*, April 17, 2012.

139. "Yemen Reels from Army's Defeat by al-Qaeda," *Arab News*, March 7, 2012.

140. "Yemen Army Death Toll from al Qaeda Assault Jumps to 185," *Jordan Times*, March 7, 2012.

141. "Yemeni Bomb Attack Kills at least 26 People in Mukalla," *BBC News*, February 25, 2012.

142. Ahmed al-Hajj, "Officials: 106 Dead in Yemen Fighting," Associated Press, March 5, 2012.

143. "222 Killed in Five Days of Yemen Clashes: Official," *Khaleej Times*, April 15, 2012.

144. "US-Trained Counter-Terrorism Forces Fight al-Qaeda in Abyan," *Yemen Post*, April 15, 2012.

145. "At Least 60 Die in New Qaeda Raid on Town," *Gulf Times*, April 10, 2012.

146. Ahmed al Haj, "Yemen: 50 al-Qaida Fighters Killed in Attack on Southern Town Suspected US Airstrike," Associated Press, April 12, 2012.

147. Associated Press, "Al Qaeda Stages Surprise Attack on Yemeni Base," *The Wall Street Journal*, May 8, 2012.

148. Qusa was supposed to film the sinking of the *USS Cole* as a propaganda spectacle but overslept and missed the attack.

149. Fawaz al-Haidari, "Yemen Army Pushing Qaeda Back," Agence France-Presse, May 16, 2012.

150. "Al-Qaeda in Yemen on the Run as Military Regains Control Over 2 of Its Strongholds," *The Washington Post*, June 12, 2012.

151. *Ibid*.

152. "Yemen Tribes Denounce Threats to Saudi Security," *Saudi Gazette*, January 6, 2010.

153. "Yemen Air Force, Troops Kill 62 Militants," *Khaleej Times*, April 12, 2012.

154. "Qaeda Suspects Die in Yemen Air Strike," *Gulf Times*, April 16, 2012.

155. See, for example, Ken Dilanian and David S. Cloud, "Yemen Sees Rise in U.S. Strikes," *Los Angeles Times*, April 2, 2012; "U.S. Drone Strike Kills 7 al-Qaeda Members in Yemen," *USA Today*, April 14, 2012.

156. Adam Baron, "Yemeni Air Force Suffers Embarrassing Crashes as Yemenis Get Angry at US," *The Christian Science Monitor*, February 30, 2013.

157. Ellen Knickmeyer and Hakim Almasmari, "Attack on Military is a Blow to Yemen," *The Wall Street Journal*, May 22, 2012.

158. Sudarsan Raghavan, "Suicide Bombing in Yemen Kills Scores at Military Parade Rehearsal," *The Washington Post*, May 21, 2012.

159. Ahmed al-Haj, "Suicide Bombing Kills Nearly 100 Soldiers in Yemen," Associated Press, May 21, 2012.

160. "Troops launch Attack to Retake Yemen City," *Gulf Times*, May 13, 2012; "Yemen Officials Say Navy Shelling Has Killed 29 al-Qaeda Militants in Southern Coastal Region," *The Washington Post*, March 22, 2012.

161. "Yemeni Army Retakes al Qaeda Bastions," *Jordan Times*, June 12, 2012.

162. Kuwait News Agency, "Al-Qaeda Withdraws from Ja'ar, Southern Yemen," June 12, 2012.

163. Mohammed Mukhashaf, "Yemen Army, in Major Victory Retakes Two Cities," *Reuters.com*, June 12, 2012.

164. "Yemen 'Set To Retake 3rd Town'," *Gulf Times*, June 14, 2012.

165. Sam Kimball, "Yemen: What an Al-Qaeda Assassination Has Exposed," *Time Online*, June 20, 2012.

166. Mohammed Mukhashaf, "Yemen Army Says Seizes Qaeda Bastion in Major Advance," *Reuters.com*, June 15, 2012.

167. "Yemen Cracks Qaeda Cell Suspected of Sanaa Attacks," *Gulf Today*, June 29, 2012.

168. "Two Killed in Yemen as Army Pursues Militants," *Saudi Gazette*, July 2, 2012.

169. "Al-Qaeda in Yemen on the Run as Military Regains Control over 2 of Its Strongholds."

170. *Ibid.*

171. "Yemen Says al-Qaeda Land Mines Killed 73 This Week," *Arab News*, June 27, 2012.

172. Associated Press, "Yemen: Landmines Kill 81 in Two Weeks since al-Qaeda Lost Control of Stronghold," *The Washington Post*, June 30, 2012.

173. Mohammed Mukhashaf, "Yemeni Force Take al-Qaeda Bastion" *The Washington Post*, June 16, 2012.

174. "Yemen Foils Plot to Attack Foreign Embassies," *Jordan Times*, June 19, 2012.

175. Ahmed al-Haj, "Senior Yemen Policeman Killed by Bomb in Car," *Daily Star*, July 19, 2012.

176. "Senior Yemen Army Officer Survives Roadside Bomb-Government," *Reuters*, July 22, 2012.

177. "Two Killed in Yemen as Army Pursues Militants," *Reuters*, July 1, 2012.

178. "At Least 22 Dead in Yemen Police Academy Suicide Bombing," *Arab News*, July 12, 2012.

179. "Yemen Foils Plot Against Embassies in Sanaa: Report," *Daily Star*, June 20, 2012.

180. Mohammed Mukhashaf, "Suicide Bomber Kills 45 in South City," *Daily Star*, August 5, 2012.

181. "At Least 14 Killed in Attack on Yemen Intelligence HQ," *Daily Star*, August 19, 2012.

182. Ahmed al Haj, "Yemen Leader Blames al-Qaeda for Attacks," *Daily Star*, October 26, 2012.

183. "Assassination Campaign Continues against Intelligence Officers," *Yemen Post*, December 17, 2012.

184. "At Least 14 Killed in Attack on Yemen Intelligence HQ"; "Assassination Campaign Continues against Intelligence Officers."

185. *Ibid.*

186. "10 Suicide Bombings Thwarted Says Yemen," *Saudi Gazette*, July 3, 2012; "Yemeni Police Arrest 54 al-Qaeda Suspects," Kuwait News Agency, July 4, 2012; "Yemen Foils Qaeda Plot, Seizes 40 Explosive Belts," *Daily Star*, August 8, 2012.

187. "Yemen Says It Foiled Sanaa Suicide Bombing Plot," July 2, 2012, available from *google.com/hostednews/afp/article*.

188. Ed White, "Nigerian Underwear Bomber Gets Life in Prison," Associated Press, February 16, 2012; Jason Ryan, "Underwear Bomber Umar Farouk Abdulmutallab Pleads Guilty," ABC News, October 12, 2011.

189. Peter Finn, "Awlaki Directed '09 Bomb Plot, U.S. Say," *The Washington Post*, February 11, 2012.

190. Sarah Wheaton, "Obama Plays Down Military Role in Yemen," *New York Times*, January 11, 2010.

191. *Ibid.*

192. Daniel Klaidman, "Drones: The Silent Killers," *Newsweek*, June 4 and 11, 2012, p. 44.

193. Sudarsan Raghavan, "Anwar al-Aulaqi, U.S.-Born Cleric Linked to al-Qaeda, Reported in Yemen," *The Washington Post*, September 30, 2011.

194. Gregory D. Johnsen, "AQAP in Yemen and the Christmas Day Terrorist Attack," *West Point Counter Terrorism Center Sentinel*, January 2010, p. 5.

195. Christopher Hefflelfinger, "Anwar al-'Awlaqi: Profile of a Jihadi Radicalizer," *West Point Counter Terrorism Center Sentinel*, March 2010.

196. Jeremy Pelofsky, "Prosecutors Say al Qaeda Leader Awlaki Directed Underwear Bomber," *Reuters*, February 10, 2012; Finn, "Awlaki directed '09 bomb plot, U.S. Say."

197. Johnsen, *The Last Refuge*, pp. 260-261.

198. Klaidman, p. 44.

199. Peter Finn and Sudarsan Raghavan, "Yemeni al-Qaeda Took a Blow but Remains a Threat to U.S.," *The Washington Post*, October 1, 2011.

200. Sudarsan Raghavan and Karen De Young, "Despite Death of Awlaki, U.S.-Yemen Relations Strained," *The Washington Post*, October 5, 2011.

201. Finn, "Awlaki Directed '09 Bomb Plot, U.S. Say."

202. Ellen Knickmeyer and Siobhan Gorman, "Behind Foiled Jet Plot, Stronger Saudi Ties," *The Wall Street Journal*, May 10, 2012.

203. Greg Miller and Karen De Young, "Al-Qaeda Plot to Bomb Airliner Thwarted, U.S. Says," *The Washington Post*, May 8, 2012.

204. Missy Ryan, "U.S. to Resume Military Training Aimed at al Qaeda in Yemen," *Chicago Tribune*, May 8, 2012.

205. *Reuters*, "Yemen Says Unaware of Alleged Plane Bomb Plots," *Chicago Tribune*, May 8, 2012.

206. Donna Leinwand Leger, "2nd Underwear Bomb Plot Foiled," *USA Today*, May 8, 2012, p. 1.

207. "Saudi King Appoints Prince Mohammad as New Interior Minister," *Arab News*, November 6, 2012.

208. "US Orders Embassy Staff to Leave Yemen," *Kuwait Times*, April 9, 2008.

209. Ahmed al-Haj, "Yemen Upholds Death Sentences in U.S. Embassy Attack," *Washington Times*, July 11, 2010.

210. "Yemen Qaeda Claims Attack on UK Envoy," *Gulf Times*, May 13, 2010.

211. Ahmed al-Haj, "Yemen: Al-Qaeda Offers Bounty for US Ambassador," Associated Press, December 30, 2012.

212. *Ibid.*

213. Greg Miller, "Brennan Speech Is First Obama Acknowledgment of Use of Armed Drones," *The Washington Post*, April 30, 2012.

214. "Secretary Panetta Interview with ABC News Jake Tapper," as quoted in U.S. Department of Defense, *News Transcript*, May 27, 2012.

215. "Yemen FM Admits Use of US Drones," *Gulf Times*, June 28, 2012.

216. Greg Miller, "In Interview, Yemeni President Acknowledges Approving U.S. Drone Strikes," *The Washington Post*, September 29, 2012.

217. *Ibid.*

218. *Ibid.*

219. Andrew Hammond, "Yemeni Debate Over Drones Emerges after Saleh's Fall," *Reuters*, October 17, 2012.

220. "US Drones Cause Political Strain in Yemen," *Kuwait Times*, May 10, 2012.

221. Ibrahim Mothana, "How Drones Help al-Qaeda," *New York Times*, June 14, 2012.

222. Andrew Hammond, "Yemeni Debate Over Drones Emerges Post-Saleh," *The Daily Star*, October 18, 2012.

223. Scott Shane, "Election Spurred a Move to Codify U.S. Drone Policy," *New York Times*, November 24, 2012.

224. Gregory D. Johnsen, *The Last Refuge*, p. 265. Please note that some sources have stated that cooperation improved after Saleh left power. See Gary Thomas, "Yemeni Intelligence Cooperation Improves after Saleh," *Voice of America News*, May 10, 2012.

225. Johnsen, *The Last Refuge*, p. 264.

226. Greg Miller, "U.S. Drone Campaign in Yemen Expanded," *The Washington Post*, April 26, 2012, p. 8.

227. "Yemen Unity Cabinet Expected Within 2 Days," *Jordan Times*, December 5, 2011.

228. Laura Kasinof, "Protesters Set New Goal: Fixing Yemen's Military," *New York Times*, February 27, 2012.

229. "Yemen Reveals 100,000 Fictitious Soldiers in Elite Military Units, Site," *Yemen Post*, December 14, 2012.

230. Sadeq al-Wesabi, "Strikes Hit Political Security," *Yemen Times*, January 30, 2012.

231. Sudarsan Raghavan, "Yemeni Air Force Officers Protest in Sign of Coming Struggle," *The Washington Post*, February 20, 2012.

232. Hakun Akmasmari and Margaret Coker, "Al-Qaeda Militants Escape Strike," *The Wall Street Journal*, April 9, 2012.

233. "Yemen President Orders Military Trial for Saleh's Rebelling Half-Brother," *The National*, April 16, 2012.

234. "Yemen al Qaeda leader Is Killed in Drone Attack," *Gulf Times*, April 25, 2012.

235. Ahmed al-Haj, "Yemen Air Force Ends Mutiny on Vow to Oust Chief," Associated Press, March 19, 2012.

236. Reuters, "Yemen Clips Saleh Son's Powers," *Saudi Gazette*, August 8, 2012.

237. Agence France-Presse, "Yemen Reforms Military, Limits Saleh Son's Power," *The Gulf Today*, August 7, 2012.

238. Ahmed al-Haj, "Yemen: 62 Troops to Be Tried Over Ministry Attack," *Daily Star*, August 16, 2012.

239. "Military Courts to Prosecute Dozens of Yemeni Soldiers," *Yemen Post*, December 3, 2012.

240. "Republican Guard Members Sentenced in Yemen," *New York Times*, December 15, 2012.

241. "Yemen leader, Saleh Son in Standoff Over Missiles," *Gulf Times*, December 12, 2012.

242. "Staff Brigadier Ali Naji Obaid Speaks to the Yemen Times," *Yemen Times*, December 31, 2012.

243. At the time of this writing, there were numerous rumors of such a transfer. See "Yemen General May Head New Unit After Army Overhaul," *Reuters*, December 23, 2012.

244. Abdurrahman Shamlan, "Military Reorganization Bid of Yemen's President," *Arab News*, December 25, 2012.

245. Elena White, "Yemen's Brigadier General Yehia Mohammed Saleh Denied He Will Run for the Presidency," *Yemen Observer*, May 2, 2012.

246. *Yemen: Enduring Conflicts, Threatened Transition*, p. 5.

247. *Ibid.*

248. Hammoud Mounassar, "Yemen Airport Shutdown After Threat from Fired General," Agence France-Presse, April 7, 2012.

249. "Yemen Reels from Army's Defeat by al-Qaeda," *Arab News*, March 7, 2012.

250. "Airstrike Illustrates Ballooning US Involvement in Yemen," Associated Press, December 24, 2009.

251. Casey L. Coombs, "Yemen to Get UAVs from the U.S.," *Aerospace Daily & Defense Report,* September 26, 2012.

252. "President Obama Executive Order Gives Treasury Authority to Freeze Yemeni Assets in U.S.," *The Washington Post*, May 16, 2012; Lolita C. Baldor, "US Preparing to Restart Military Aid to Yemen," Associated Press, March 10, 2012.

253. "Obama Promises Justice for Christmas Terror Plotters," *CNN.com*, January 2, 2010.

254. Noah Browning, Abigail Fielding-Smith, and Roula Khalaf, "Yemen Deployed US-Trained Special Forces," *Financial Times*, June 3, 2011.

255. "Money Flows Again," *Aviation Week & Space Technology*, July 2, 2012.

256. "Yemen, Jordan Discuss Anti-Terror Fight," *Gulf Times*, May 11, 2010; "Jordan Ready to Help Yemen Restructure Army," Petra-Jordanian News Agency, May 16, 2012.

257. "Hadi Shakes Up Army," Sanaa *Yemen Fox*, December 20, 2012. Note that Yemen Fox is a Sanaa based independent news website managed by the Sanaa-based al-Shunu Foundation for Press in the Media.

258. "Jordanian Military Committee Helps Interior Ministry with Internal Security Restructure," *Yemen Times*, January 17, 2013.

259. Riad Kahwaji and Barbara Opall-Rome, "Rebuilding Iraq's Military," *Defense News*, June 2, 2003, p. 1.

260. "Jordanian Facility to Train Regional and International Forces," *National Defense*, August 2006, pp. 22-23.

261. Pierre Tran, "Conference News: Center offers Global Special Ops Training," *Defense News, SOFEX 2006 Conference*, March 27, 2006.

262. For a more detailed exploration of these issues, see W. Andrew Terrill, *Global Security Watch Jordan*, Santa Barbara: CA: Praeger, 2010, pp. 42-44.

263. An extremely good book on this subject is James A. Russell, *Innovation, Transformation, and War: Counterinsurgency Operations in Anbar and Ninewa Provinces, Iraq, 2005-2007*, Stanford, CA: Stanford Security Studies, 2011.

U.S. ARMY WAR COLLEGE

Major General Anthony A. Cucolo III
Commandant

*****

STRATEGIC STUDIES INSTITUTE
and
U.S. ARMY WAR COLLEGE PRESS

Director
Professor Douglas C. Lovelace, Jr.

Director of Research
Dr. Steven K. Metz

Author
Dr. W. Andrew Terrill

Editor for Production
Dr. James G. Pierce

Publications Assistant
Ms. Rita A. Rummel

*****

Composition
Mrs. Jennifer E. Nevil

www.ingramcontent.com/pod-product-compliance
Lightning Source LLC
Chambersburg PA
CBHW081253040426
42453CB00014B/2398